BORN IN 1970?
WHAT ELSE HAPPENED?

RON WILLIAMS

AUSTRALIAN SOCIAL HISTORY

BOOK 32 IN A SERIES OF 35

FROM 1939 to 1973

BOOM, BOOM BABY, BOOM

BORN IN 1970? WHAT ELSE HAPPENED?

Published by Boom Books. Wickham, NSW, Australia

Web: boombooks.biz
Email: jen@boombooks.biz

© Ron Williams 2013. This revised edition: 2022
A single chapter or part thereof may be copied and reproduced without permission, provided that the Author, Title, and Web Site are acknowledged.

Creator: Williams, Ron, 1934- author
Title: Born in 1970? What else happened?
ISBN: 9780648771685

Some Letters used in this text may still be in copyright. Every reasonable effort has been made to locate the writers. If any persons or their estates can establish authorship, and want to discuss copyright, please contact the author at jen@boombooks.biz

Cover images: National Archives of Australia:

A1200 1189294 Ardlethan Miner

A1200 11664583 Waratah Spring Festival 1970

A1200 11664824 Children singing carols

A1200 11869357 Surfer girl

INTRODUCTION iii

CONTENTS

MORE RIGHTS FOR BABIES	3
OUR ASIAN FOREIGN POLICY	4
CONSCIENTIOUS OBJECTORS	26
HI-JACKING IS VERY POPULAR	29
SHOULD ABORTIONS BE LEGALISED	35
DOCTORS FEES AND THE AMA	38
ANOTHER LOOK AT VIETNAM	43
SAVING FOR A HOME	57
HOW GOOD IS OUR HEALTH SYSTEM	68
TRADE UNIONS UNDER SCRUTINY	72
GREEN BANS AND STRIKES	83
THE CRICKET TOUR BY SOUTH AFRICA	87
URBAN SPRAWL	116
THE FUNERAL INDUSTRY	119
SOME THINGS NEVER CHANGE	131
POOR TREATMENT OF VETERANS	136
TO BE OR NOT TO BE	148
THE TAMBORINE BRIGADE	161
MERRY CHRISTMAS - IF POSSIBLE	173
SUMMING UP 1970	183

BORN IN 1970?

IMPORTANT PEOPLE AND RECORDS

Queen of England	Elizabeth II
Prime Minister of Australia	John Gorton
Leader of the Opposition	Gough Whitlam
Gov. General	P Hasluck
Pope	Paul VI
PM of England	Harold Wilson
	Edward Heath
President of America	Richard Nixon

WINNER OF THE ASHES
1968	Drawn 1 - 1
1970 - 71	England 2 - 0
1972	Drawn 2 - 2

MELBOURNE CUP WINNERS
1969	Rainlover
1970	Baghdad Note
1971	Silver Knight

ACADEMY AWARDS
Best Actor	John Wayne
Best Actress	Maggie Smith
Best Movie	Midn't Cowboy

INTRODUCTION

This book is the 32nd in a series of 35 books that I have researched and written. It tells a story about a number of important or newsworthy Australia-centric events that happened in 1970. The series covers each of the years from 1939 to 1973 for a total of 35 books.

I developed my interest in writing these books a few years ago at a time when my children entered their teens. My own teens started in 1947, and I started trying to remember what had happened to me then. I thought of the big events first, like Saturday afternoon at the pictures, and cricket in the back yard, and the wonderful fun of going to Maitland on the train for school each day.

Then I recalled some of the not-so-good things. I was an altar boy, and that meant three or four Masses a week. I might have thought I loved God at that stage, but I really hated his Masses. And the schoolboy bullies, like Greg Favvell, and the hapless Freddie Ebans. Yet, to compensate for these, there was always the beautiful, black headed, blue-sailor-suited June Brown, who I was allowed to worship from a distance.

I also thought about my parents. Most of the major events that I lived through came to mind readily. But after that, I realised that I really knew very little about these parents of mine. They had been born about the start of the Twentieth Century, and they died in 1970 and 1980. For their last 20 years, I was old enough to speak with a bit of sense. I could have talked to them a lot about their lives. I could have found out about the times they lived in. But I did not. I know almost nothing about them really. Their courtship? Working in the pits? The Lock-out in the Depression? Losing their second child? Being dusted as a miner? The shootings at Rothbury? My uncles killed in the War? There were hundreds, thousands of questions that I would now like to ask them. But, alas, I can't. It's too late.

Thus, prompted by my guilt, I resolved to write these books. They describe happenings that affected people, real people. In 1970, there is some coverage of international affairs, but a lot more on social events within Australia. This book, and the whole series is, to coin a modern phrase, designed to push the reader's buttons, to make you remember and wonder at things forgotten. The books might just let nostalgia see the light of day, so that oldies and youngies will talk about the past and re-discover a heritage otherwise forgotten. Hopefully, they will spark discussions between generations, and foster the asking and the answering of questions that should not remain unanswered.

The sources of my material. I was born in 1934, so that I can remember well a great deal of what went on around me from 1939 onwards. But of course, the bulk of this book's material came from research. That meant that I spent many hours in front of a computer reading electronic versions of newspapers, magazines, Hansard, Ministers' Press releases and the like. My task was to sift out, day-by-day, those stories and events that would be of interest to the most readers. Then I supplemented these with materials from books, broadcasts, memoirs, biographies, government reports and statistics. And I talked to old-timers, one-on-one, and in organised groups, and to Baby Boomers about their recollections. People with stories to tell came out of the woodwork, and talked no end about the tragic, and funny, and commonplace events that have shaped their very different lives.

The presentation of each book. For each year covered, the end result is a collection of short Chapters on many of the topics that concerned ordinary people in that year. I think I have covered most of the major issues that people then were interested in. On the other hand, in some cases I have dwelt a little on minor frivolous matters, perhaps to the detriment of more sober considerations. Still, in the long run, this makes the book more readable, and hopefully it will convey adequately the spirit of the times.

Each of the books is mainly Sydney based, but I have been deliberately national in outlook, so that readers elsewhere will feel comfortable that I am talking about matters that affected them personally. After all, housing shortages and strikes and juvenile delinquency involved all Australians, and other issues, such as problems overseas, had no State component in them. Overall, I expect I can make you wonder, remember, rage and giggle equally, no matter where you hail from.

BACKGROUND STORIES FROM 1969

The Vietnam War. This really started a decade ago, as a civil war between the North and the South of Vietnam. Both of these two forces wanted to get rid of the Dutch colonialists, but the North wanted to replace them with a Communist state, while the South wanted a more liberal state, roughly along the lines of America.

So, two armies, and lots of volunteers under very different banners, started a civil war. It was low-key at first, but it developed over the years, until about 1965 it was reaching full-scale war. By then, the USA, and Australia, were involved with the South, while the Reds, China and Russia, were supporting the North.

In 1960, nobody in Oz cared one bit about another civil war in a far-away country they had never heard of. This was still the case, more or less, in 1965. But after that, our Australian leaders started talking about sending our Regular Army troops to fight and be killed in Vietnam.

Then, a bit later, they started talking about conscription, and forcing our young men to do the same. And finally, they introduced a lottery, based on date-of-birth, that demanded that a fair share of these 20-year-olds leave whatever they were doing, and go to the fighting fields for the purpose of kill or be killed. That got the population concerned.

Parents and families and friends and others hated this. Why go to nowhere and kill other young men that you had no idea of? Why take my son, give him a gun, and send him off to be killed? A very formidable opposition to the war immediately formed.

But an equally vociferous support also developed. These Russian and Chinese Reds want to capture all Asia and come also and get Australia. They will start in Vietnam, and roll down the Pacific, and never be content **until the Red flag was flying over Tasmania**. The place and time to stop the Red menace was in Vietnam now.

Let me briefly say that by the end of 1969, the divisions over the war had only deepened. As our men, young and older, were killed, the arguments and fights and public demonstrations grew and grew. Wise people kept their mouths shut, others opened up wide, and someone was always ready to put their rhetorical fist in them.

Near the end of 1969, half of Australia supported the war, and the other half hated it. Then, in Vietnam, a Company of American soldiers entered a native village of Mai Lai and destroyed it, killed the men and assaulted the women, and burned it down. This was filmed and shown on US television. Many witnesses testified that it had happened, and gradually it was found that other villages had received similar treatment.

Americans at home were horrified, and so too were Australians. Sentiment in support of the war dropped, and by year's end, probably only 40 per cent of our population supported continuing to fight the war.

Further news from Vietnam. As we proceed through this book, I will not give a description of any military matters, or dwell of the wins and losses in battles. In fact, I will restrict myself to talking about the social issues that the war raised back in Oz. I hope, though, that you will remember occasionally that **the war was going on, and on, even though I might not mention it for a Chapter or two.**

The man on the moon. Another big event of 1969 was the landing on the moon by three US astronauts. For a while before that it was obvious that something big in space was about to be completed, with the US and Russia pulling off more and more daring feats.

Finally, **the Race to the Moon was over**, and the US was the winner. It was a great coup, and the entire world sent its congratulations. America responded with all the modesty that was expected of it.

But it did not mean that the Space Race was over. Soon after, the Russians had their space moments, then the USA, then the Russians, and on and on it went. It seemed that the rivalry between the two nations, both on land in Vietnam and now in space, was destined to escalate at an ever-increasing pace. It seemed too that US paranoia about Russia and the Reds had no limit, and doubtless, visa versa.

This paranoia has continued into 1970 and beyond, even to the present day. Now and then, there has been a small thaw and unqualified peace has threatened to break out. But, inevitably it seems, someone somewhere takes affront at something the other baddie has done, and all-out rivalry and thoughts of violence and destruction come to the fore.

As we proceed through 1970, I will point out some of these thoughts as they become obvious.

Catholic versus Public schools. For about a century, a big question that bedevilled politicians and civic leaders was who was to pay for the education of school children. By 1969, the many disputes had settled down to one major question.

Two separate school systems had grown up. One was made up of State Schools, and this was financed by the separate State governments. The second was financed and supported by groups that were independent of the State, and the Catholic Church was by far the biggest component of this.

The question that still was not answered was the same: **who should pay for this?**

The State-schoolers obviously think the State **should not**. And that should be the end of that. If the Catholics argue - as they do - that the State should pay for the Catholic schools as well, they counter that the State system is there for any one who wants it. If the Catholics want a separate system, that's well and good, but it is they who pay for it, and not the taxpayers of the State.

The Catholics argue that they need a school system that allows religious instruction as the norm, and that the teachers should be monks, brothers and nuns. They want to have prayers as part of the normal school day, and occasional religious services during the school day. Such provisions are not consistent with a State school.

The arguments get a lot deeper and more devious than my simplification, but readers will pick up more as we proceed. The issue had been a hot one in 1969, and it won't cool off in 1970.

Growing acceptance of Asia. Twenty five years ago, at the end of WWII, many Australian people had come to accept the Japanese for their part in the War. But I need to hedge that statement in so many directions. For example, some relatives of the dead, or the maimed, or those imprisoned, had said years ago that they would never forgive, and they held that attitude until the day that they died.

Others said that they had come to realise that the Japanese were just people like ourselves, and as a nation had been seduced into a war that they had no power to stop. So they were coming to accept the former bitter enemy.

Some were swayed by financial interests because Japan was becoming a major customer of our agriculture and minerals. As well, recent trade fairs had opened our eyes to the range of desirable and novel products that were just waiting to be brought. These list of different attitudes to Japan could go on and on. But in general, our active hostility to all things Japanese was falling quickly.

Aborigines in society. The average person's attitude towards Aborigines had changed a lot in the last 20 years. Without spelling out any details, let me just say that the Aborigines in general were now seen as an under-privileged body of people who need help to integrate into the Australian way of life.

I need to add that this was not universally accepted and quite a few people still clung to the long-held views that Aborigines were decadent and inferior and would never change. I also point out that probably no white, no matter how well intentioned, had any idea of what should actually be done to help the situation.

But, reiterating, the attitude of the average person was much more supportive and friendly that it had ever been before.

Licensed clubs. In 1953, there were 393 registered clubs in NSW. In 1969, there were 1446. The growth in numbers was similar in all the other States.

To be registered meant a Club could serve liquor and food, had to have reasonable facilities, and could install a fair number of poker machines. Throughout the 1960's, every hamlet in this broad nation started its own club, and just now these small units were being gobbled up by the bigger ones.

So a few problems were on the horizon. Were the bigger clubs serving small communities? Were the clubs generally extracting too much money from members via the pokies? Were clubs becoming a focal point for criminal activities?

MY RULES IN WRITING

Note. Throughout this book, I rely a lot on reproducing Letters from the newspapers. Whenever I do this, I put the text in a different font, and indent it a little, and make the font somewhat smaller. I do not edit the text at all. The same is true for the News Items at the start of each Chapter. **That is, I do not correct spelling or if the text gets at all garbled, I do not correct it. It's just as it was seen in the Papers.**

Second Note. The material for this book, when it comes from newspapers, is reported as it was seen at the time. If the benefit of hindsight over the years changes things, then I might record that in my Comments. **The info reported thus reflects matters as seen in 1970.**

Third Note. Let me also apologise in advance to anyone I might offend. In a work such as this, **it is certain some people will think I got some things wrong. I am sure that I did**, but please remember, all of **this is only my opinion**. And really, **my** opinion does not matter one little bit in the scheme of things. **I hope you will say "silly old bugger", and shrug your shoulders, and read on.**

So, OFF WE GO, ready to plunge into 1970.

JANUARY NEWS ITEMS

The newspapers, along with the rest of the nation, were on summer holidays. **So they were in no mood for work.** They avoided some of this once again by filling the first page of the New Year with news of the **Queen's Birthday Honours....**

To my uneducated mind, there was this year **hardly any one I recognised**. There were 18 new Australian Knights created, and the only one that stood out for me was **Rod Miller, Chairman of Millers Brewing**. The other person that rang a bell, or a gong perhaps, was from England, and he was Noel Coward....

But it makes me wonder: Year after year I look at this list, and year after year I am not on it. **What am I doing wrong?**

In all Australian States, **abortion was illegal. Backyard operators proliferated**, and many of these were described as butchers. Police were supposed to crack down on these persons, but turned a blind eye....

In Victoria, six doctors have registered complaints and are prepared to **give testimony against illegal operators**. The Government has appointed a Queen's Counsel to investigate. It is known that at least **30 Police Officers will be called** to answer charges that they took bribes to not perform their duty. It is alleged that one of them was paid $153,000 from one woman abortionist. It is also alleged that such payments go back at least 20 years. Also, that they were paid in all States.

The Council at the NSW country city of Orange is about to make a big decision. Two years ago, **English perch were introduced into Lake Canobolas to supplement the trout there**. But the perch are multiplying rapidly and out-eating the trout....

The Council will **decide whether to poison all the fish in the lake**, and then re-stock it only with trout. The poison to be used is Derris Dust, well known to gardeners at the time. We await the Council's decision with *baited* breath.

Our newspapers were full of anti-Russian and anti-Red propaganda. Every second day, the front page of the *Sydney Morning Herald* carried a story about the bad Reds doing something that we should all be worried about. For example, on January 9th we were told that Russia was stepping up their production of long-range missiles. The USA was just behind them. Why they needed these was not explained.....

Maybe it was to confirm that the Reds were all dangerous guys, and to **keep us fearful of the future atrocities that would never happen**....

My own attitude was, and is, that **they were foolish scare stories not worthy of regular mention**. I will not willingly talk about them again.

MORE RIGHTS FOR BABIES

The NSW Government will soon introduce legislation that will give more rights to 18-year-olds. They will be able to buy houses and land, enter hire-purchase agreements, and make wills. Previously, they needed the signature of a trustee or guarantor, usually a parent. The Premier said that it will be the first step "towards emancipation of 18 to 20 years-olds".

At the same time, discussions are being held between the States and Commonwealth examining whether the right to **vote in elections should be extended to all these youths and girls**. After all, it is argued, the males can be conscripted and sent to Vietnam, where they are shot at and too often killed. Give them the right to vote against such rules if they choose.

There are other considerations, though. Do the youngsters have the knowledge, the judgement, the balance to soberly cast votes in National elections? A solid group of people said they do not. But this group was up against some real arguments and also very telling slogans, like **"OLD ENOUGH TO DIE, BUT NOT OLD ENOUGH TO VOTE"**.

In the next year, though, the matter was decided in favour of extending voting rights.

It is worth noting that parental consent for marriage was still need in about half the States. In these cases, the age was generally set at 18.

OUR ASIAN FOREIGN POLICY

Archbishop Sloane, the Anglican Archbishop of Sydney, complained that Australia had no clearly defined policy towards Asian nations. He went on to say that Australians are "insular, self-contained, complacent and provincial".

He was right on both charges. We had no broad policy. And we were a very insular lot. **But it could be argued that these were not vices, but rather they were virtues.**

Letters, R Caldwell. Historically, foreign policies have invariably signified a method of cajoling, bribing, coercing or defeating your neighbours in order to increase the wealth or power of your own country. However successful they may have been for a time, they all ended in disaster. Examples in contemporary history are Hitler's eastern expansion policy, Japan's co-prosperity sphere, Italy's African colonisation, Napoleon's hegemony over Europe. The most successful was Britain's balance-of-power policy, which has now become a thing of the past.

In this uncertain world, a clear-cut policy towards each and every nation is an impossible thing to ask. After all, the United Nations was set up ideally to solve international quarrels, and to render unnecessary countless national policies. It has failed, but no more disastrously than did the separate policies.

Perhaps the Archbishop means that we should simply state in a clear, loud voice: "We want to like all of you, so let us all be friends and co-operate." This naive appeal would display an attitude, but cannot be called a policy.

Foreign policy nowadays seems to be an hour-to-hour affair. No statesman can dare to commit his government over a long period.

Letters, Tom Collins. How can we have a single foreign policy towards Asians? **On the one hand, we have Japan, an ex-enemy that no one trusts and half the population hates.** On the other hand we have India that sacrificed its men to save us in the War, and we are on friendly terms with.

To formulate a foreign policy is to place us in a straight jacket. In this rapidly changing world, we need to be nimble, and to change as the world swings this way and that. We also need a policy that differentiates between friends and foes, and what else there is that makes one nation different from another.

Then there was the true statement that we were insular. Mr Caldwell returns to the fray.

Letters, R Caldwell. As to our shortcomings, the Archbishop has described these in words that ring more like compliments than insults. Insular? Anyone who lives on an island is insular, whether he be broad or narrow-minded. Would he be a better man by being continental? Self-contained: this sounds rather laudatory, like independent, self-reliant. Complacent: to be pleased with yourself and your environment - if any of us have yet reached that happy condition, we are to be envied, not blamed. Provincial? Looking at the smog-ridden, congested, nerve-racked conurbations overseas, I think it's rather pleasant to be provincial.

Credibility shattered, I presented an argument in your columns that if it had taken over half a million or so troops to bolster up the ARVN in a failing fight, then how in heaven's name could the ARVN hope to survive let alone win once this support was withdrawn? I also pointed out that the much vaunted aims of containing Communism were being given away under the cover of a new and unfounded optimism.

Another writer adds his bit.

Letters, Rudolf Moore. I would like this nation even more than I do currently if it was more isolated and insular. Every real problem that we have, in every sphere of life, comes from overseas. I would like to see the rest of the world lock us in and forget us.

Comment. This idea has a lot to recommend it, but what happens when we run out of Morris Oxfords, and all that stuff?

YOU CAN'T PLAY IF YOU ARE BLACK

South Africa was always in the news because of its **policy of Apartheid** . This was designed to keep the blacks and the whites separate from each other. It had a long history. Blacks are blacks, and whites are white, and never the twain shall meet.

Not all whites supported this policy, but those who did argued that whites, mainly from Holland and Britain, had built up the nation, and had brought peace and prosperity to what had previously been fighting tribes bordering on poverty and consumed with diseases. Now these blacks wanted to get pelf and power away from the whites. To keep them at bay, Apartheid supporters wanted the whites to continue on as a privileged class, and the blacks to be excluded.

The opposing blacks wanted power, and land and all property, to come under black control. Some wanted this to be done without compensation and perhaps violence, others wanted it done by gradual, peaceful means. But the end result was to be the same. Namely, to expel the whites and have the blacks take over.

With this brief and doubtless defamatory explanation of a very complex problem, let me refer to the current South African controversy **as it appeared in Australian sport.**

Under Apartheid, black players were excluded from playing in international teams that had been selected to play overseas. For example, quite a few cricketers were good performers, but were not selected, solely because they were black. In Australia, Cricket and Rugby Union were the sports that were most conscious of this ban.

I present below two Letters that give some idea of how the arguments were framed.

> **Letters, Barry Cohen, MP for Robertson.**
> The Prime Minister of South Africa said that he would not allow multi-racial sports teams from the Republic to make overseas tours.
>
> I was reminded once again of the recent outburst by Sir Wilfrid Kent Hughes, MP, the self-appointed spokesman for the Federal Parliament on sporting matters, when he advised Australian sporting bodies to ignore mounting pressure to break off sporting relations with South Africa and told them "not to bring politics into sport."
>
> The facts are quite straightforward. It is South Africa's vicious Apartheid policy that is the initiator of the opposition to South Africa's inclusion in world sport. **When South Africa decides to include people in**

her sporting activities, both at home and abroad, without the prerequisite of a white skin, **then South Africa will find herself welcome among the sporting nations of the world.**

I would also hope that those who echo Sir Wilfrid's sentiments would ponder on the possibility of Lionel Rose, Evonne Goolagong or Ian King ever displaying their talents in South Africa.

Letters, G Mant. I would like to support Mr Barry Cohen on his remarks on Apartheid in sport. As he says, the likelihood of Evonne Goolagong, Lionel Rose or Ian King ever appearing in South Africa is remote. One hopes Mr Darby has also warned his cricket pupils from Taiwan that if they ever reach big-time international status, they will also be prohibited from playing in South Africa because of the colour their skins.

I was utterly disgusted to read this week that non-whites (Africans and Indians) were barred from even **watching** the match between Australia and North-Eastern Transvaal at Pretoria. This is Apartheid gone mad.

Australian apologists declare that politics should be kept out of sport. So they should, but first let South Africa set the example.

Surely by playing cricket under their present Apartheid rule we are condoning it?

Letters, Tony Coutts. So now it might have got to the stage where **no teams** from Australia or South Africa can tour to each other's country. We can't have blacks and whites playing in the same game. Surely that's not cricket.

Let me say that I have no objection to a white South African team touring Australia, even playing Test Matches. But they should be labelled as the South African **Colonialists** team, and not the South African team. Surely a team that represents only 5 per cent of the home state cannot play as a national team.

INCOME TAX

Even back in the long-distant days of 1970, people did not like paying tax. And, believe it or not, there were some people who would work hard to create vile schemes to avoid paying their fair share. What utter villains.

Still, there were lots of others who suggested changes to the tax system would be proper. The writer below offers two such.

Letters, M Lloyd. Our new Treasurer in 1970 should and must be looking for ways and means of reducing the rates of personal income-tax. I think it is appreciated by all parties that the existing situation should not be allowed to continue.

I suggest that there are two new taxes which Mr Bury could introduce immediately on a Commonwealth-wide basis with a view to relieving the tax rates for those earning salaries and wages.

First, I suggest that the betting turnover-tax applicable to bookmakers on racecourses be applied to sharebrokers. Without any doubt our stock exchanges are the greatest gambling dens in Australia at the present time. A betting turnover-tax applied to share transactions should be a considerable source of revenue and is well merited. It is appreciated that such a tax would not be over-popular as all the "good" people play the stock exchange.

Secondly, I feel that it is long overdue that a capital gains-tax be introduced in Australia. It is ridiculous that salary and wage earners pay the bulk of the taxation when all those who have inherited capital and have made capital gains pay no tax at all on the appreciation of their capital assets on their sale. This tax would bring in a considerable volume of revenue and would equalise the position in relationship to salary and wage earners and those making profit on capital transactions.

Comment. The first suggestion was made at a time when the Stock Markets across the nation were in an enormous bubble caused initially by the discovery of nickel near an outback place called Poseidon. Fortunes were made as nickel stocks rose sharply each day and other stocks rose on the back of them.

But of course, the boom burst, and it burst savagely. So, the stocks all fell in value. Mr Lloyd might like to think about what would happen with his suggestion then. Would all the taxes paid on rising stocks be refunded when the stocks fell?

The second suggestion is for a capital gains tax. Alas, Mr Lloyd's suggestion was accepted by the Taxation Department, and it now bedevils the lives of everyone with non-housing assets.

I suppose it is too late to ask Mr Lloyd to keep his suggestions to himself.

Second comment. A notorious English actor, Warren Mitchell, was visiting Australia on tour. He lamented "People here are more concerned with nickel than with the Arts."

MORE ON TAXATION

But there is a lot more to be said on taxation. No matter how far in time you go back, and no matter how far into the immediate years, taxation is always in the news. In fact, I could easily fill a book with the Letters from this year alone on the subject. Let me give you another Letter from January.

Letters, J Venn. I have recently perused a circular issued by the Commissioner of Stamp Duties in which it was advised that the concession which has been enjoyed for years by small clubs and the like whereby they enjoyed the privilege of having a cheque account on which the cheques were exempted from stamp duty is to be withdrawn.

It is obvious that now the Government is to expect some loss of revenue from land-tax, which is paid only by persons who own valuable land and are therefore of some influence, some means has to be found to recoup that loss from some other source. Where else would the Government look but to the small club where it is thought the influence is smaller?

Therefore, it has been decided as from January 1, 1970, **that clubs** like schoolboys' cricket clubs, suburban ladies' tennis clubs, youths' Soccer clubs, ladies' church guilds and similar bodies **will be taxed** five cents on each cheque they issue. The only clubs now exempted are those of a charitable nature and RSL clubs. Of course the influence which these clubs have on the Government does not need any elaboration. Perhaps Mr Askin does not realise that the small clubs will now be closing their cheque accounts and in future will either pay their accounts by cash or by money order and in the latter instance the poundage will go to the Commonwealth Government so that the NSW Government will still be the loser.

Why doesn't the NSW Government wake up and realise that the small clubs in many cases cannot afford the extra burden? They have recently been forced to pay receipts tax, too, and now we have this additional burden, a tax on what they pay, as well.

Comment. Someone said once that there are only two things that are certain in life. Namely, death and taxes. I am not so certain about death. But from reading thirty years of newspapers day by day, and also reading far ahead right up to the minute, I agree fully with the comment on the certainty of taxes. I suppose that other issues do attract as much attention, over an extended period, but I am struggling at the moment to recall what they are.

CRICKET IS MORE THAN A GAME
Mr Michael Darby was the elected MLA for Manly. He had a lot of original ideas that he was always prepared

to share with the public. Some of these were quite sensible. Some of them were not. Right now he made public a suggestion for **the use of cricket in the field of international relations**. Writers critique this idea below.

Letters, (Mrs) H Wilson. Mr Darby said "I do think that we've got to bring the tropical world into our way of life." The ultimate in creating this great program of international understanding has, in Mr Darby's reasoning, been the commencement of an exciting educational program to which our Federal government has allocated $2,500 and equally patriotic citizens have donated $8,500, to teach the activity which made the British great....cricket.

Who are we teaching? Chinese students from Taiwan. Why? Because "If the Chinese nation is to be made great, then they must learn cricket, too."

I wonder if the supporters of this great cause of winning China to cricket would just as "ardently" support the cause of bringing our own Aboriginal people into our way of life.

Unlike Mr Darby, I believe we should give all subjects equal opportunities to receive an education. This is not available to Aboriginal children who need to be taught how to re-establish their empire, not by conquest, which seems to be a fearful ingredient of the non-cricket-playing races, but by giving them some of the institutions that made us great - schools, hospitals, full employment, etc.

Letters, Archie Jackson. The point of cricket is to promote the idea that we can engage in enterprises with fairness and consideration for others and still thrive. We do not care who wins, but *rather we thrill in the game itself.*

Everyone will find that, as we go through life, serious cricketers and followers will give you a fair deal. They will not cheat, they will be there when they are needed, and they are not there to beat you down.

If we can induce our Asian and Pacific friends to think this way, and to do business this way, our relations with them will be ever so much better.

So, let us keep up our Tests with England, but also promote teams and Tests with Japan and China and Asia generally.

FEBRUARY NEWS ITEMS

The Roman Catholic Pope is not too popular in **Holland at the moment**. At least, not among priests, many of whom last week made a request that **priests no longer should be compelled to be celibate**. They had been thus controlled for centuries, but they thought that in the modern world the time had come to be more liberal....

But not so, said the Pope. Tough it out, was his message. And there was no hope for the future. Celibacy was part and parcel of being a Catholic priest, and it **somehow made the Church a better place**, the Pope said.

The British Government will soon allow **the use of marijuana for medical purposes**. It will be the first Western nation to do so. Note that Australia trailed Britain in this respect, and indeed in some States even now the use of pot for such purposes is persistently monitored and controlled.

Bubble trouble. Stock Exchanges around the nation are working with Governments furiously on creating legislation that will curb **the huge amount of speculation in shares** that has captivated the population. It is right now in the middle of the **Poseidon nickel boom**, and prices of all mining stocks are daily showing big gains. It will surely end in disaster....

But the regulators are just nibbling at the edges. **They do not want the boom to stop really**, they are making too much money from commissions and Stamp Duty. So they are talking about better education for the public as their main policy for restraint. **A fat lot of good that will do** when half the population are making 10 per cent gain every week.

Bruce Gyngall, an executive of the Seven TV Network, is forecasting that it will become possible for customers to **use the telephone to dial up programs of their own choice.** He thinks this will not happen for about ten years. **It seems a bit far-fetched to me.**

Another challenger for the America's Cup has slid down the slip-way. *Gretel II*, financed by Frank Packer, is about to undergo racing tests. A little-known sailor, **Jim Hardy, is to try out for helmsman**....

Gretel II and the previous challenger **Gretel** will soon be shipped to Newport in the US. They will race against each other there, and then *Gretel II* will compete against a French vessel for permission to **race against the American choice.**...

This is a very expensive venture. I suggest that those involved should save their time and money. The Americans have a mountain of money, and they lead the world in technology....

I tell you emphatically that Australia will never win the America's Cup.

TOBACCO IS NASTY BUT NOT DANGEROUS

The use of tobacco products was close to its peak. Australia was a cigarette-based society, and for long there had been little thought about somehow, or for some reason, restricting its permeation of our society.

But there were a few people who were just starting to make their protesting voices heard.

Letters, Craven Awful. We had some visitors to our home last weekend. They were old friends and very welcome. They had a cup of tea with us in our lounge room and left after an hour. All very pleasant.

After they left, however, I realised that they had entered our home, and without any thought, lit up their smokes. We hastened to get them ashtrays. And they smoked almost non-stop for an hour. There was nothing surprising in this. This is just standard practice.

But I now realise that this should not be standard practice. We are non-smokers, and we do not enjoy cleaning up the ashes and butts. We do not like the smoke in our faces and eyes, nor the smokers' coughs of our friends, nor the smell of smoke on their clothing and ours as well. In fact, we would like never to play host to smokers again.

But people of all walks of life come to our home, and take it for granted that all of this is acceptable.

We do not know what can be done about it without giving offence to people we do not wish to offend.

There were other Letters creeping into the Press, and they were coming from quite different perspectives.

Letters, F Lewis. Many daily train travellers will have read with interest Wednesday's report that 60 per cent of Gosford-Sydney passengers favour non-smoking carriages.

In Victoria it was recently announced that smoking may be banned in Melbourne suburban trains because of offence to non-smoking passengers and its contribution towards uncleanliness. Previously the ratio of smoking compartments in Melbourne trains had been reduced from two-thirds to one-third after a survey of the numbers of passengers smoking.

These findings should be given consideration by the New South Wales Department of Railways. Daily observation suggests that the proportion of smokers nowadays is in fact considerably less than one in four, whatever it may have been in the days when the existing allocation in Sydney trains was fixed as three smoking carriages to one non-smoking. In view of the Gosford survey, non-smoking accommodation should be increased to at least one carriage in two.

Another cause of complaint is the method of marking non-smoking carriages. The only means of identification are flimsy paper stickers pasted on to carriages. Very often these are removed, effectively converting the carriage to a smoking carriage.

Permanent no-smoking signs in suburban carriages would protect non-smokers against the frequent disappearance of these stickers, as well as relieving the Railways Department of the manpower committed to affixing and removing the stickers at depots.

Letters, W Stern. I note that the new Boeing 747 aircraft coming into service will have "smoking" and "non-smoking" compartments, and I feel that attention to this problem on our domestic airlines is long overdue.

As a businessman using domestic airlines fairly regularly, I find it most objectionable to be forced to inhale tobacco fumes, especially where food is being served. Even if my immediate neighbour is not a smoker,

I still find I have sore eyes and an itchy nose for days after a flight.

As most trips (Sydney-Melbourne, Sydney-Brisbane) last only an hour, surely the heaviest smoker would find little hardship in abstaining from smoking for this short period.

In view of the fact that health authorities recognise smoking as a proven health hazard, airline authorities should provide "non-smoking" sections so that non-smokers are not inconvenienced. If this is not possible, the Department of Civil Aviation should ban smoking on domestic airlines without delay.

The idea of non-smoking carriages on trains prompted a reader to suggest non-smoking compartments in aircraft.

Letters, R Mead. My suggestion has no bearing on transport, but is of equal importance: smoking while visiting hospital. Visiting hours are brief enough, and if a visitor cannot do without a cigarette for the short time he is in a ward, then he should leave the building to smoke.

Surely the health and wellbeing of his own relative or friend, and the other patients, should be more important.

Comment. A much greater menace was the health hazard barely mentioned in Mr Stern's Letter. The link between smoking and cancer of the lungs was just starting to filter through in the UK and the USA, but it had scarcely made a dent here.

And it would be decades and decades before the cancer link was accepted as a fact by the smoking community in general. In 1970, cigarette advertising was everywhere, on billboards, in glossy magazines, in the daily papers, on the packets. If you wanted glamour, and sophistication, look to the American films where actors were puffing away in half the scenes as they were shot.

Children could buy the gaspers "for their dad", Mums were encouraged by the Women's Magazines to throw off their yolk and light up. Young boys collected empty cigarette packets and stored and traded their treasures. It was Paradise for the marketing gurus of the tobacco industry.

THE COUNTRY IS STILL THERE

We live in a wide brown land, and much of our population is spread along the coast, and a hundred inland cities. Between these, we have all sorts of graziers and farmers and miners and others who between them make a fortune for the nation, but who are scarcely heard of in the Press and the evening TV.

Now, at the end of January, this nation gets back to business, and starts churning out news at a furious rate. In that hurly burly, when the news is centred around the big cities and nearby, it is easy to forget that the inland even exists. So, every now and then throughout this book, I will present a small reminder that our Outback is still there and, believe it or not, the neglected news from there is just as interesting as that from the cites. Well....almost.

Letters, M Sawtell. City people have no idea how terrible those dust storms can be that are now raging up in the inland. The Simpson Desert is the main cause of that dust. You can see the wind blowing the loose sand off the tops of the sandhills. In 1900 when I was a drover's boy on the Birdsville Track, and I used to sleep out on the ground in a swag, the wind would blow a heap of sand up against my back.

The sand storm would cover over houses, fences and stockyards. The wire-netting rabbit-proof fence between South Australia and Queensland was covered by sand and another fence was built on top of it. In about 1898 Joe Clark, a drover from Sandringham Station, lost a mob of 200 cattle in a storm on the Birdsville track. The only way to lessen the severity of those terrible storms is to grow more trees. The inland is seriously deficient in trees, but the ordinary Aussie would sooner cut a tree down than plant one.

Letters, R Roper, Abschol Trustees.
It was not very pleasant to read your news story about Mr Bils being refused admission to an Aboriginal Reserve in the Northern Territory. If this were an isolated instance it would still be the cause of a great deal of concern. However, it is not an isolated instance. Many people have been prevented from visiting Aboriginal Reserves throughout Australia.

It is claimed that these laws are designed to protect Aborigines. They seem more designed to protect European Governments from having their actions looked into. In both the Northern Territory and Queensland, the two worst offenders, university lecturers have been prevented from undertaking much-needed research by governmental restrictions on their activity.

Only two years ago in New South Wales an Aboriginal friend asked me to come and visit him on the north coast of New South Wales. As I happened to be nearby, I went to the reserve but was warned off by an officer of the old Aborigines' Welfare Board. Even if I had been a close relative I would still have had to get a white man's permission to visit the reserve.

It is intolerable that in 1970 Aborigines still do not have control over their own futures and not even over who can visit them. In the last week there has been considerable publicity given to the disgraceful condition of Aboriginal affairs in Queensland. Abschol has called on the Commonwealth Government to intervene in Queensland to safeguard the interests of the 50,000 Aborigines who live there.

The Commonwealth must also surely give consideration to intervening wherever the rights of Aborigines as citizens of Australia are taken away. The Northern Territory is purely a Commonwealth responsibility and they cannot allow Mr Glese, the Director of the Welfare Board, to have more power over the everyday activities of the Aborigines than we permit anyone to have over Europeans.

CONSCIENTIOUS OBJECTORS

Whenever this nation went to war, there were a number of young men who did not want to go off and kill other young men. If, however, conscription was the order of the day, they were drafted and had to explain why they did not, and would not, fight. The reason, they said, might be that they had religious objections to doing this, or perhaps their objections come from moral principles.

Whatever the case, the authorities considered that they had to co-opt or punish them in some way, and they devised ways to make them uncomfortable, and to make them pariahs to the general population.

Arguments over their fate did not change much over the years. Those that supported the conscies rejected all arguments that they should be compelled to kill. Their opponents said that if the nation decided that we were at war with someone else, then we had the duty to prosecute the war and that young men were the right persons to do that.

In WWI and WWII, the Australian public were united in the opinion that we should go to the aid of Britain. But in this Vietnam war, the nation was split about equally and so there was more sympathy for the conscies than there had ever been before.

In previous wars, the Australian army, backed by Governments, had sometimes allowed the conscies to join the army, but not to bear arms. In some cases, they were used as stretcher bearers, sometimes to just clean the latrines. **For this current war, many of them were easily dealt with. They were simply sent to prison.**

The woman below tells us how she feels.

Letters, E Mowbray. On Saturday, February 28, I visited one of my sons, who is serving a prison sentence for opposition to the National Service Act. He is the third member of our family to be fined and gaoled. These men are no different from many other young Australians who oppose the present legislation and who, as a result, have continuous pressure brought to bear on them to change their conscientiously held beliefs.

The basis of their attitude is a conscientious objection to a "conscripting" Act and the firm belief that a man is inescapably responsible for his own actions. Whatever differences of opinion are held, there can be no dispute as to the sincerity of these men. No reasonable person believes any longer that any man puts up with the treatment they receive, year after year, because he wants notoriety or has some longing for martyrdom.

While opposing the present legislation these men, by their training and day-to-day activities, have endeavoured to prepare themselves to serve humanity in some of the many fields where such service is needed so greatly.

Nothing has strengthened more my personal conviction that it is entirely wrong to bring pressure to bear to cause men to stifle their conscience than this recent visit to Long Bay. For young men, determined to use their talents and abilities for good, this kind of experience is appalling. To be shut behind locked doors only causes frustration, disappointment and bitterness, while wasting their ability. They realise that, finally, this is the kind of action our Government takes and our community allows.

Comment. The nasty term "conscie" stuck with people all their lives. There was always someone who would pop up out of the blue with the knowledge that some person had "refused to serve" in some war. It was like the other vicious appellation "scab" that was used to brand a member of a Trade Union who refused to strike at a time that the masses were striking.

These were terms that stank of malice. The man was always thus open to attack, and so too was his family, and on that score alone, non-strikers had to be very concerned about falling out with the mob.

HI-JACKING IS VERY POPULAR

Flights in long-distance airlines, always with some risk at the time, were becoming more hazardous because of the growing practice of discontented people hi-jacking the plane.

Fortunately Australia had missed this craze so far, but in most of the world, individuals and small teams with guns were taking command of flights, and demanding to be flown to destinations in the strangest parts of the world.

When they arrived, they were generally captured and dealt with by the authorities, and it is hard to recall a single adventure that ended in success for the hi-jackers. Authorities world-wide are tightening up on protocols and notification procedures, so that it can be expected that soon incoming hi-jacked planes will always be met with displays of force.

Still, at the moment, the malcontents are enjoying notoriety and are making other travellers very nervous.

Letters, M Krumbeck, Executive Secretary, Australian Federation of Travel Agents. The Australian Federation of Travel Agents welcomes the news that a bill to tighten Australian controls on aerial hijackers has been introduced in the Senate.

Although the areas in which these activities have been occurring are not directly involving Australian travellers, there is no guarantee that the "popularity" of hijacking will not gain impetus.

Such a development would have a serious impact on tourist passenger air traffic and coming at a time when increased load factors on aircraft are becoming vital together with current Australian promotional campaigns would be most inopportune.

It is hoped that other Governments will take similar action in an endeavour to eliminate this undesirable and dangerous practice.

TWO BRIGHT IDEAS

Letters, P Darby. On behalf of the "toehold commuters" who fight their way on to the trains at Central, I congratulate the State Government in finally going ahead with plans to increase the number of **double-deck carriages**.

But why are they calling tenders for motorised units? Surely at least three trailing carriages could be bought for the price of two motorised ones.

Although I sympathise with the drivers in their argument over the condition of the single-deck, motorised carriages and with the engineers who are trying to keep them running, the customers' comfort should come first. I doubt if the purchase of, say, 70 trailing double-deck carriages would exceed the cost of 53 double-deck motorised carriages. Furthermore, wouldn't it be more logical to increase the capacity of all trains by 50 per cent rather than half the trains by 100 per cent?

Letters, J Dooley. But for the use of the modern jet-powered lifeboat, the 16 lifesavers saved from treacherous seas during the South Curl Curl surf carnival may have drowned. One wonders, therefore, why flippers, another modern safety aid, are not standard equipment for surf lifesavers.

Flippers give greatly increased support when treading water and add speed to swimming. They can be put on or removed quickly and when not required, such as when walking out into the surf, could be simply clipped to a belt worn by the lifesaver.

As time and support in the surf are so critical to saving people from drowning, the use of flippers would surely be a tremendous aid.

A FAIR QUESTION

Questions were again raised this week about who does run this country. Is it the Government or is it **the Trade Unions?**

BAD NEWS FROM THE FRONT LINE

The grim news came through that **eight Australian soldiers had been killed in Vietnam. Twenty-nine others were wounded.** This added to the steady stream of death and disaster reported regularly.

MARCH NEWS ITEMS

Police are trying to track down **a Good Samaritan male who offers late-night lifts to drinkers after closing hours**. Once they get into his car, he offers them a beer that is drugged. They become unconscious, and he drives to bushland, strips them, robs them of whatever they are carrying, and **leaves them naked in the bush....**

Three victims have reported so far. Police have a description of a man who is average in all respects, except for **the fact that he is "well-spoken"**.

The Stock Market boom was drawing large crowds to **public stock market galleries**. In these, punters could watch the movements on the Boards as the shares were traded....

In Sydney, as from March 1st, watching crowds were regulated. Forty watchers were allowed in for a maximum of 10 minutes, and the queue waiting was always about 100. **A policeman was occupied full-time in regulating the swarms....**

But the Nickel Boom got a bit of a shock on March 3rd. Tasminex, a red hot favourite among the tipsters, came in with an annual report that said that they had discovered no nickel on their leases....

The shares in Tasminex had earlier dashed to $90 on January 23rd. **On March 3rd, they started selling at $17. But after the announcement, they fell to below $7.

Three State Governments have announced **enquiries into Tasminex.**

Maybe the Nickel Boom will not go on forever?

There is a lot of big talk coming from the US after their successful landing on the moon last year. President Nixon has just mentioned the possibility of a **manned landing on Mars by 1986**....

This did not happen.

A Mayne Nickless Security Van **picked up $588,000 from a Sydney bank for delivery to customers**. The three guards stopped to have lunch in their van in the shopping centre at a Sydney suburb....

They opened the door to put their rubbish in a bin. Three other men were waiting and, flourishing pistols, took over....

They tied up the drivers, and **took the money into a waiting car, and escaped**. Police are investigating this big-haul daring robbery....

Three days later they had made no arrests. But they had discovered that **a blue-print for the robbery** had been **on sale among prisoners in Sydney's Long Bay prison last year**.

SHOULD ABORTIONS BE LEGALISED

The Editor of the *SMH* touched on a delicate topic. He argued that there were certain activities that the population considered basic and that **no amount of interference by authorities or police**, and no amount of social persuasion, **could stop people from using them**.

He cited examples of gambling, prostitution, drinking after hours. He quoted from America where prohibition led to criminal activity "greater than the world had ever previously seen." He said that the main result of attempts to suppress them was to corrupt the police officers who were involved in the futile task of suppression.

He then turned to abortion in Victoria. Police there were under attack for their leniency in enforcing the many laws against abortion. Every day there was a new headline in the Papers telling of woeful excesses that were being ignored.

The only course of action, said the Editor, was to legalise abortion. This, he says, has already been done in Britain and South Australia. To do otherwise would be to deliver many desperate and unhappy women into the hands of racketeers and incompetent practitioners. And it would guarantee that the law, and all its agencies, would continue to be brought into disrepute.

There were millions of Australians who thought this was bad advice. All major religions were against it, and they led to the argument that abortion was the taking of human lives. There was no worry then about **when**

a foetus became a human as there is fifty years later. Instead, opponents of abortion said that once conceived, any termination of life was just plain murder.

So, a majority of the population still persevered in the criticism of pregnant women outside marriage. In some cases, the situation was hush hush for as long as possible, then if finance was available, the mother was spirited away to "a cousin's place in Sydney". In other cases, the miscreant was taken to a back-yard scoundrel and there a worrying and dubious procedure was performed. I remind you that in most States, abortion by licensed doctors was illegal, and it was the lack of policing of this that had the critics up in arms.

There was plenty of correspondence around that.

Letters, J Freebury, Abortion Law Reform Association, NSW. It is perfectly evident that some of the politically powerful regard the issue as trivial. The present situation is intolerable. It makes cowards and hypocrites of doctors. Why should they have to refuse to help a woman by saying, "It is the law"...?

We must concern ourselves with the most fundamental rights of children - to be wanted, loved, and given a reasonable start in the world.

It seems ironic that society requires the most careful checking and screening of persons who want to adopt children, and at the same time indiscriminately requires parents to go ahead with births they do not want.

Birth-control clinics must be allowed to advertise their existence and services. This is a "must." The present archaic laws must go. After the first year of the Abortion Act in the UK several orphanages were closed. Surely this alone shows the great need for reform of the law.

The proper question is **not**, "How can we justify an abortion?" but, "How can we justify a compulsory pregnancy?"

Letters (Mrs) D Weeks. It is not commonly revealed that the Catholic Church has not always taken the extreme view that it does today and that, at varying times and under other Popes, it regarded abortion, before and after quickening, in very different categories; also, under English Common Law, prior to 1803 abortion was not deemed a punishable offence unless committed after quickening. It was merely a misdemeanour.

The question arises, however - are our legislators in NSW enlightened enough to ensure that we become one of the few civilised communities where a woman's ownership of her own body is accepted, not as a means of population control as in Japan, but as her basic human right?

Letters, (Miss) I Ellis. I strongly object to your editorial of March 2. It is disappointing that a responsible newspaper should supinely surrender to the avant-garde section of the permissive society.

Drafting of laws which would assist those who wish to destroy human life can never be justified.

Have we yet tried (to quote your editorial) "the best preventive measures" and "the most enlightened social education"? Not, I think, to the limits possible. We must press for these remedies unremittingly.

Comment. Over the years, the arguments have become more sophisticated as medical knowledge has changed. And the influence of the Churches has dwindled. But the debates remain the same. **At some stage, the foetus acquires the status of a human being. Where is that point? And then the real decision, can it then be aborted?**

DOCTORS FEES AND THE AMA

The battle over fees to be paid to doctors rages on. For over a dozen years, Governments have been talking about some form of compensation for patients when they amass fees for services for doctors and specialists. **Schemes have come and gone**, and right now it seems that a formula might have been found that satisfies the medicos and also the public, and also the Government that will foot the bill.

In short, in fact, in very short, the idea of a common fee has been proposed by the Federal Government. So that a patient will be charged a certain fee for service, and as well, the Government will pay a bit more to the doctor.

There are many different and competing ways to do this in practice. But the common basis for these fees is that all payments are decided in advance by Government. That means that different doctors cannot charge higher rates than others for the same service.

You can easily see how this would upset some medicos. The swanky physician prescribing pills in Melbourne's Toorak builds his practice on charging a higher rate than the struggling family doctor servicing Oodnadatta. A doctor delivering a baby in Sydney's Saint Vincent's Hospital in Sydney will expect a larger payment than a doctor in a gunyah in Port Macquarie.

Objections abounded to this common fee concept. In particular, the version that said that **specialists should only get the same fee as a general practitioner** for providing a particular service got every specialist in the nation offside. They had good arguments for opposing this new proposed rule. Among these, they could claim that they had studied longer, had more knowledge, and that the patients referred to them were the difficult ones that general practitioners could not handle.

So, on all these points, and many others, the issues of fees to be paid for treatment could be best described as "under discussion."

I present part of an Editorial in the *SMH*, and two Letters below. They are just to give you a small idea of how the battle was raging.

> **Editorial.** It is the differential rates for specialists and general practitioners on which the scheme will sink or swim, however awkwardly. It means the difference between a comprehensive benefit scheme for all or one standard of medical service for the wealthy and another for the poor.
>
> Why should a person so ill that his doctor considers he should be referred to a more highly qualified specialist be penalised for his misfortune? Why, if he cannot afford the specialist, should he be forced to accept a lower standard of medical care? It is true that with no difference in costs patients will probably prefer specialist treatment, but in many cases only because the profession over the years has made him believe he will receive better care.
>
> Surely this is a problem which the medical profession can overcome by the referral system. Patients must have some trust in the advice of their general practitioners or they would not consult them.

Letters, General Practitioner. It seems to me that any suggestion of an attempt to compel any practitioner to reduce his present fee in line with a common fee (when his present fee, related to the hours worked and the cost of maintaining the service provided, gives no more than a reasonable net return) should be re-examined before it gets under way.

Letters, Western Suburbs GP. Your editorial of March 12 indicates that you do not appreciate the basic objection general practitioners have to the Commonwealth Government's proposed medical scheme. This is understandable, as the Commonwealth Government and even some sections of the AMA are similarly ignorant.

General practice has been gradually running down for some years, due to an inadequate influx of new graduates; mainly the result of the strong influences to specialise they experience during their student and resident years. We have the position that the average age of general practitioners in this State is increasing; it is now over 40 years. About half of the country GPs are English graduates - most of them refugees from a type of medical practice which held little interest for them; they are willing to earn less provided they can obtain satisfaction from their work. Will they stay here if they are reduced to medical clerks? What will happen to the country people if a significant proportion of them return to the UK? And will new graduates enter general practice if we are officially made second-rate doctors?

One must appreciate that it is usually the better type of GP who likes to do some surgery, obstetrics, take his own electrocardiographs or perform other procedures which are not beyond the limits of reasonable competence. I do little surgery and obstetrics and receive less than 5 per cent of my gross income from these procedures; if I were prevented from indulging in those which interest me, a great deal of fulfilment would be taken from my work and I would not hesitate to quit general practice for some less demanding and less remunerative manner of earning my living.

This section of my practice is the icing on the cake - the break from the everyday routine of minor and often monotonous complaints. The miracle and drama of childbirth is the best tonic I know.

I cannot contemplate any effective or personal medical service without GPs, but this is what you are advocating; not immediately, but as the present GPs become older and fewer, this will happen.

Comment on an unrelated matter. Notice in the last Letter, that the role of a GP was different from the present time. A bit of surgery, a birth, a bit of machine operating. Jolly good fun. Different from the pill-pushers and go-see-a-specialist or two that we see nowadays.

A DIFFERENT LOOK AT VIETNAM

Again, I remind you that I am deliberately not giving you the gory details of the war in Vietnam. Instead, I am just picking out a few particularly significant matters here and there. I think the Letter below fits in here.

Letters, J Gray. The Minister for Education, Mr Cutler, is reported to have said recently that he will not permit discussion of the Vietnam War in NSW High Schools because, he says, "children must be taught to obey the law of the Commonwealth of Australia."

In some contexts this sentiment of obeying the law is admirable, but what law of the land forbids discussion of the Vietnam War? Is there not actually a law specifically permitting freedom of speech and discussion? Or does this not apply in High schools?

True, there is a law that demands that boys in senior years must register for National Service (and at present this means the war in Vietnam) before they are very much older, but, surely, no law forbidding the discussion of why this is so? On the contrary, if Mr Cutler had the true interests of the young people under his charge at heart he would encourage such activity as extremely important.

If he fears the discussions would be one-sided and biased against the war, why not have the Education Department formally organise them and ensure that both sides get a "fair go"?

Or does he really feel that the Government's case (with which, by the latest Gallup poll, only 40 per cent of Australians agree) would not stand up to informed and disinterested analysis?

These young people have every right to be informed of all the pros and cons since it is they who are more involved than anyone else - they are the ones who must risk their lives. I urge Mr Cutler to reconsider his position.

Comment. I agree that teachers in general were opposed to the war. And that many of them would try to lead the youths in their classes to a similar position.

But it is hard to believe that our 17-year-olds would be so passive that they would let any teacher get away with that. Especially in this era of violent protest against the war. The classrooms might erupt into chaos, but it is unrealistic to believe that any teacher could indoctrinate the children and sway opinion one way or another.

Second comment. It is hard to know what the percentage of support for the war was at any time. Most of the polls were deliberately deceptive and partisan, and poorly conducted. But Jane Gray's estimate that only 40 per cent of Australians now supported the war is pretty close to my own estimate.

Certainly the figure had dropped in the last few months as the May Lai revelations proceeded, and as Americans lost their enthusiasm. And in Australia, the death and casualty toll rose every day, and what were the tangible gains? Were the Reds tiring, were they letting up? Not one bit, as far as we could see.

So, 40 percent will satisfy me for the moment.

FREE LIBRARIES TO GO?

Over two decades and more, citizens across Australia had campaigned for free municipal libraries. These hopefully would be paid for by local Councils, and funded by a universal charge on ratepayers.

At times, the arguments had been bitter, Why should I pay for library services when I can't even read? I only want children's books. I only want women's books.

There will be no books on vigaro. Will they carry books reporting fairly on Communism?

But, support from communities was very strong, and often-reluctant Councils by now were generally supportive of the idea of free Council libraries.

But there was still some rear-guard action. The Letter below relates to one of the most affluent communities in the nation.

Letters, (Mrs) P Ryan. T Phillips' Letter instances the protests of ratepayers generally kept ignorant of councils' agenda. Better, surely, the belated protest than such general apathy as exists in Kuring-gai municipality today - even when we are informed of council's intentions.

Early in January there were reports in our local paper of the council debating to abolish our free library service; true, some aldermen walked out in disgust, but there was no effort on the part of ratepayers to support them. Since then, the council has ceased the operations of the mobile library van which served all the primary schools and several shopping centres throughout the municipality, completely closed down one branch library (at Wahroonga) and imposed lending fees on books which have been hitherto, and in all other municipal libraries still are, borrowed free of charge.

Since Alderman Rickard wrote showing how the library was one of the many services the council has sabotaged under the guise of "pegging the rate," I have been looking in vain for some form of protest, at least from the many librarians among the ratepayers.

Surely we need some explanation of how Alderman Turner and co. have been able in one fell swoop to circumvent the Free Library Act of 1944.

Comment. Fortunately, the free-library movement was able to withstand the various and numerous challenges, so that free municipal libraries are now accepted as part of the ordained essentials of a civilised society.

AN EARLY VOICE FOR CONSERVATION

Here is a theme that is familiar to all.

Letters, (Mrs) R Lawrence. I refer to the headings "One of world's greatest tourist spots," "It's unique," "Every sort of fishing thrill." All these statements are, of course, true of that phenomenon of nature, the Great Barrier Reef.

However, I fail to understand the "ostrich" attitude of the tourist authorities who ignore the destruction wrought by the Crown of Thorns starfish, or try to whitewash the issue with bland statements that "nature will cure itself," as in a recent television report.

According to a report by the Australian Academy of Science the Crown of Thorns starfish is impossible to control except in a few selected tourist areas. If this happens and we have only remnants of the 1,250 miles of reef surviving it will be a disgrace to our country.

Surely the tourists who have enjoyed the wonders of the Reef should be among the first to plead for its preservation, if only they are told the truth.

Comment. Our society has grown familiar with the damage reported to the Reef from the Crown of Thorns.

But it is interesting to note that this Letter was written about 50 years ago, and it is the only one that I have seen, writing about that topic in the newspapers, for the next 20 to 30 years.

MODERN MEDICAL MIRACLES

A man, who received a heart and double lung transplant last week, died from lung rejection. The **miracles of organ transplants had just started**, but there was as yet no guarantee of success.

APRIL NEWS ITEMS

It's all very exciting. At the end of March, **the Queen and Prince Phillip landed in Australia**. Their children Charles and Anne came along for the ride, half fare. They landed at Mascot in Sydney, and shortly after were at **the Royal Easter Show**....

The major noticeboard at the Show displayed the upcoming events for the afternoon It read:

12.33 Final of Junior Axemen.

1.30   Grand Parade.

2.30   The Queen....

Informality was the order of the day. There were few barriers, the Royals could wander as they pleased, and they appeared to be under no time-table pressure **A good start to the Royal Tour.**

The dispute over fees for medical services rages on. At the moment, specialists and general practitioners are at each others' throats. Proposals are that fees actually paid to a medico for **a given service will be the same for both camps....**

If you had a gall bladder removed, then the GP and the specialist would get the same amount. But, argue the GPs, **everyone would go to the specialist** because he is seen as having the greater skills. The GPs can see that their own practices, offering 300 services of the same type, **would go out of business**. The battle continues.

The Great Train Robber, the Brit Ronald Biggs, had been on the lam for months and months. He was often reported to be in South America, Melbourne, and other exotic locations. This week, the *Sun-Herald* said **he had been in Darwin for the last week**, and had flown to Indonesia in a chartered plane when he was fingered. The story was given **by bounty hunters who try to anticipate his every reported footstep**.

A woman in Gundagai was given **some poppy seeds 17 years ago by her aunt**. For the next 17 years, she has grown the poppies in her garden, and been proud of the fact that the flowers were bigger and more vigorous than normal poppies. **She has given away lots of seeds** and delighted in seeing the flowers from these brightening up the gardens of neighbours....

Then she bought a magazine and was shocked to see her poppies pictured as being of the opium variety. She sent seeds to the Agriculture Department, and, sure enough, **they were opium poppies**. The town will now be scoured by the authorities to ensure eradication. The lady, it was decided after deliberation, **will not be prosecuted** under any of the pertinent Acts. But she was issued with a good-behaviour bond and a stern warning.

The Queen is about to visit Wollongong on the NSW South Coast. The Palace has announced that **the Mayor will be promoted to Lord Mayer.**

SUNDAYS NO LONGER DEAD

At the Melbourne Cricket Ground last Sunday, a crowd of 30,000-odd people gathered to watch a match of something resembling football. It was to be played between two teams of delusionals who thought themselves to be either Tigers or Lions. But the Royals had a jersey too, and they drove in, did a circuit of the ground, speeches were made, and everyone then watched the ensuing punch-up.

This was all very exciting. **The Royals watching a footie match, along with the plebs.** It did not happen very often. But even more exciting for the fans was that this was **the first time** that the game of Australian Rules football was licensed to play on the ground on a Sunday....

For two decades, various sporting bodies had tried to open their gates for Sunday **paid** sports. They had been met by pitched opposition all along the way with obstruction from Churches and traditionalists. Gradually, the opposing forces had been vanquished, and now, at the MCG, this was the sweetest victory of all. **The curse of the Sabbath was officially broken.**

CHEAP FLIGHTS TO KOREA

A plane, flying from Tokyo, with 93 passengers aboard, and bound for Seoul in South Korea, was hi-jacked en route by 16 radical Japanese students. They wanted to fly to North Korea. The pilots headed in that direction, but the North Koreans did not want this unannounced visitor, and fired on it. The pilots secretly arranged for it to land in Seoul as initially intended.

When it got there, it was met with a staged reception. A sign proclaimed "Welcome to North Korea", and every flag and sign at the airport that would identify it as Seoul was stripped from sight. South Korean military staff were dressed in North Korean uniforms, hostesses and pilots could be seen wandering round in NK uniforms as well. When the plane landed, it was met by authorities carrying 15 bouquets of flowers.

But the students were suspicious. They demanded to see multiple copies of posters of the North's President, abundantly displayed in the North. But there were none in the South, so the charade was stopped after five hours.

The bargaining started. Refuel the plane and let it leave, or it will be blown up was the threat. The students agreed to release the starving passengers if a particular Japanese Minister of the Government would become a hostage instead. 46 hours after the incident started, the plane was cleared to leave, and North Korea indicated it would release the passengers and return the aircraft after it landed. But more hiccups occurred so the drama went on.

So after more than three days, the passengers and crew were flown to Pyongyang Airport in North Korea. There the Minister was already in NK, and the exchange was carried out. The passengers and crew were free to fly to their original destinations, subject to the whims of the NK Government.

The students were no so lucky, however. The Government did not want mobs of Red Army Japanese students flocking there in the future, so it made it clear that the students were no welcome. They disappeared out of the news cycle and I cannot find them anywhere.

Comment. The whole ordeal took four days. Lots of sub-dramas happened. The male passengers had their hands tied behind their backs for the entire period. Women passengers, including one inevitably pregnant, fainted at times, one man's father died on hearing of the hijack. On the other hand, several passengers shook hands with the Japanese as they left the aircraft,

It surprises me that Hollywood never made a movie about such dramatic events.

Second comment. As I mentioned earlier, hi-jacking was popular at the moment. Some people who had a political problem thought they could resolve it by a hi-jack and ransom, some wanted someone else released from prison and again tried ransom, others were browned off with their job or their girlfriends. Many drunks in American got on the wrong plane, and demanded to be flown to the right place.

There was no clear pattern. So the intending passenger had to keep this danger at the back of the mind in deciding on a flight. In 1970, when planes were not so reliable, and when big crashes happened somewhere every second week, the combined risks were small but tangible.

DAYLIGHT SAVING AGAIN

Right now, around the year 2020, daylight saving is widely accepted as beneficial to Australia. Gone are the old arguments about the curtains fading fast, and the dairy cows not letting down their milk. We all expect that when October comes, we lose one hour of sleep and we don't get it back for about five months. We all know that leaves us tired throughout Summer, but we accept that as the price that we pay for the other benefits of daylight saving.

I have to point out that none of the above applies to Queensland. They have accepted for donkeys' years that such savings were not for them, and have steadfastly ignored it, staying out of line with the other States.

In any case, for the rest of Australia, daylight saving has become so accepted that readers might find it surprising that it was not always the case. Let me illustrate this with the Letter below. It is from a person in Pymble in NSW, and obviously not in a period when the savings were obvious. Nor does Mr Wilson live in Queensland.

Letters, L Wilson. Another summer has now passed with the mainland States being denied the advantages of daylight saving.

A vigorous campaign last summer generated unprecedented publicity and interest in the issue, so much so that the State Governments decided to have a meeting on the matter on December 10 last. The outcome of this meeting was rather nebulous and apart from a statement by Sir Henry Bolte that he could be interested in discussing the possibility of daylight saving with New South Wales, not a word has been said since.

The success of the idea, if it hadn't already been proved in all other industrialised countries in the world for periods exceeding 50 years, has been demonstrated conclusively in Tasmania for three summers, and in Thredbo alpine village. Yet our State Governments have been procrastinating and vacillating on the issue for 25 years. Unless action is taken promptly, we will again be told that it will be too late to do anything for next summer.

The undoubted advantages of daylight saving do not have to be detailed again, but it would appear that the objections stem essentially from misunderstanding. This has been proved in all Government inquiries in other States and countries.

The advocates of daylight saving do not ask that the practice be foisted on an unwilling public, as happens with much Government legislation. We simply want an opportunity of demonstrating by a trial period that daylight saving is acceptable and practical in this country. NSW and Victoria can indeed introduce it without the co-operation of the other States.

Comment. It seems strange today, about 2023, to hear Mr Wilson having to argue **for** daylight saving. But over the last 100 years, the arguments for and against have generally shifted back and forth, so it would not surprise me if **by the year 2040, daylight saving was back in fashion again. Though, I add, Queensland will still resist.**

You think I am wrong? Well.... check me out in 2040.

PRINCE PHILIP CAN'T PLEASE EVERYONE

Letters, I Russell. The Duke is at it again. This time he has to insult a profession that takes a pride in its appearance, neatness and dignity, the undertakers.

His remarks quoted in the "Herald" of April 2: "Students," gasped the Duke. "You look like a lot of undertakers," were apparently made to a group of bearded university students at a reception where he approached the students and asked what political party they were from. I would like to point out to the Duke and others that the students more than likely looked more like the "dashing young naval officers of the 40s" who flaunted beards such as his Royal Highness and his relatives grew during their naval careers.

It would be interesting to know why no funeral directors or their assistants were invited to any of the Royal occasions, for from what I know of them they are jolly good types. Their fingernails are clean, their hair is cut, clothing pressed and they are not given to passing inane comments.

Comment. The Prince tries hard to be informal. Probably he tried harder in Australia where formality and Class are not so apparent.

But no matter what he does, there is always someone who takes exception to something he says.

SAVING FOR A HOME

Young married couples were having trouble getting their deposits ready for their first home. All the normal deterrents were there and on top of that the Treasurer had just announced an increase in lending rates.

Letters, B Tregenza. The Federal Treasurer says that any economic restrictions placed on the community are going to hurt someone. Fair enough; young marrieds don't mind taking their share. But it seems to me that it's this very group which bears the brunt of every effort to tighten the economy.

If interest rates must be increased and if young couples must find a greater percentage of the purchase price of a house before they can raise credit for the balance, at least Real

Estate prices should be pegged. The only adverse effect this would have would be to reduce the tremendous profits developers, steel manufacturers, etc., are making from the real estate and building industries.

Today, a young married couple living on the average male weekly wage hasn't a hope of being able to save the monthly increase in the value of land, let alone sufficient to be able to put down even a 50 per cent deposit on a block. Those who have already started the struggle for home ownership face a harder battle. Those who haven't yet started will find it almost impossible while the present price spiral is allowed to continue.

Unlike Mr Cope, I don't advocate an introduction of price control in general, but certainly some measure of control on prices of land and building is necessary, rather than a straight-out increase of interest rates and tightening of credit.

Comment. As this Letter shows, there is nothing new in young people having difficulty in raising their deposits. In my own case, it took three years of deliberate saving before we had the nerve to go to the Commonwealth Bank and crawl to the manager, He told us to go away and save for another two years. We did that, and he told us to come back in another two years.

The point I am making is that young couples starting out now, about the year of 2020, who are complaining about how hard it is to get a loan to build a small mansion, are much better off than their forebears. Good luck to them all, and I hope the bankers of the world can help them out soon. But it would grate on me less if they would not make such a fuss over **the Mickey Mouse limitations now imposed**.

ABORIGINAL CUSTOMS IN A WHITE WORLD

Over the last decade, the legal and social station of Aboriginal people in Australian society had been improved a lot. All Governments, including the Federal, had introduced legislation to improve the position of Aborigines, and had made large financial budgets for this purpose. At the same time, society in general became quite sympathetic to Aboriginal causes. The change in attitude of the white man towards the black was very big indeed.

That is not to say that all the old prejudices had gone. Nor to say that all black people were treated equally by all whites. But the improvement was quite palpable, and the genuine hope of the white population was that it would continue. The big problem, though, now in 1970 and then in the year 2020, was how to do this.

But going back to 1970, this Letter below paints a picture of some of the forces and customs that mitigated against change. It also asks many alarming questions.

Letters, J Zube. According to your paper, a 14-year-old Aboriginal girl, protesting against tribal traditions, was, as a result, brutally beaten by the village leader and found no help when she appealed to the white police and magistrate.

The girl, Rita Galkama, was the wife of the former village leader. After his death tribal traditions fixed her status as the "inherited" wife Number 3 of the next village leader, a 42-year-old man.

Understandably, she protested. After the traditional tribal punishment for refusing to become the new leader's wife - a beating in which her "husband" tried to break her leg - she went to the white police for help. The case came to court and a Stipendiary Magistrate decided that the leader and "husband" was guilty of assault. Nevertheless, as a concession to Aboriginal law he did not convict him.

Should we deny her the protection of our family law which is more in accordance with human rights? Can we rightly ignore her demand to be no longer subjected to tribal law and tribal jurisdiction - a system more than 10,000 years old? Should she be subjected to this second marriage she did not desire or should the SM have annulled this tribal marriage? Should we have granted the girl asylum or should we have sent her back to suffer further punishment by tribal elders?

But what about the little girl when she returns after the Court case? How will the tribal community receive her? I and others with common sense would fear for her liberty and safety. The "Herald" could find out whether she is threatened in either way and could, find her a temporary home and finally, through appeals to the reader, a permanent home in a more civilised environment which respects at least some of the basic human rights.

The new legal principle which should have been developed and upheld in this moving case is: As "white" Australians dominating in this country, we should nevertheless bow to the application of Aboriginal tribal law among all those who still prefer it - but we should allow individuals to opt out of it and should help them in any way if they try to do this.

Herald Letter writers are vocal over most issues. They can always find something to fight about, or to debunk, or laugh about. **But with the Letter above, there was not a single response printed.**

It cannot that it be that people were not concerned. I suspect that it was because, despite the positive feelings towards Aboriginals manifest over the last decade, people were not yet ready to face up to talking about the obvious problems raised. And because none of them had any significant answer. **Look at the above Letter. I can tell you, I most certainly can't even start.**

Can you?

SPEAK UP, MAN

Letters, M Eardley-Wilmot. The televising of her Majesty's visit to Parliament House, Canberra, only accentuated the mediocrity of public speaking in Australia.

Our Prime Minister, quite unabashed, read from notes, occasionally lifting his head to relieve the strain on his neck. Our Deputy Prime Minister was equally supine but mercifully somewhat briefer. It was left to the Leader of the Opposition, even if fluffing a few lines, to speak off the cuff.

Not one of the three introduced or attempted to introduce a note of humour and each was content to rely on the same old platitudes and innocuous inanities for which such occasions are unfortunately renowned.

The Queen looked bored, as well she might, while the Duke, God bless him, appeared vaguely amused. If such occasions have to be re-enacted it would be preferable if they were not televised live, as the art of public speaking is most assuredly dead.

Comment. Over the years, following WWII, the oratory of our leading politicians swung wildly. Ben Chifley was a strong speaker, forceful and very much to the point when he spoke ad lib. But he read his prepared speeches, and then he was quite unemotional and uninspiring.

If Ben Chifley was dull, Arthur Calwell was dull, incoherent, and the epitome of an old-fashioned Labor politician.

Bob Menzies, by complete contrast, was a brilliant orator. He excelled in front of a heckling audience, and was sometimes brilliant in his speeches in Parliament.

After him, it was all downhill. Until we get to Gorton, who was as dreary as can be. But, looking into the 1970's, Gough Whitlam was a spicy, vigorous, and most competent speaker, not quite up to the Menzies standard, but still very good.

Second comment. Second rank politicians here have generally been pretty bad also. In general, **we suffered badly in comparison to overseas speakers for the whole post-war period right up to 1970**. Both the Poms and the US ran rings round us.

THE BEATLES ARE BUST

Paul McCartney has announced he wants out mainly to spend more time with his family. He may or not return to the stage, and he may or may not continue to write songs with John Lennon. But in any case, it will not be for a couple of years at best.

GOOD NEWS FOR THE BUSH

A judge in the NSW **country city** of Lismore has said that **he will not take any more divorce cases emanating from Sydn**ey. He said that "smart lawyers" are bringing their cases to Lismore to **avoid publicity** and because they are heard more quickly. **Not any more, he promised.**

MAY NEWS ITEMS

Oh Goodie. US President Nixon has directed **American forces in Vietnam to go across the border into Cambodia.** His aim is to take out North Korean forces that are massing there. "This is not an invasion" said a US statement. "It is merely an **incursion** and should be over in about eight weeks." **The Cambodian Government was not aware of the incursion....**

Comment. This incursion was bitterly opposed by the US Democratic Party, and by those who wanted the Vietnam war finished.

May 4th. The Royal Family flew out of Sydney at the end of a five week tour right round Australia.

At Kent State University in Ohio, a group of 2,000 students were marching towards a force of National Guardsmen when a few Guardsmen panicked and fired live ammunition into the leaders. **Four of them were killed, and seven wounded and 2,000 were terrified**....

Students across America demonstrated against Nixon's sending of forces into Cambodia. Some of the demos were violent....

President Nixon described the students as "kooks, bums, paranoids and social mis-fits." This **did not go down well with American students** and supporters.

Two big sporting events are due soon. The first is a **tour of England by the South African team**. **The second is the Commonwealth Games**, which involves the entire Empire...

But most African nations and India are saying that **they will not attend the Games if the South African Cricket team goes ahead with the tour**. They argue that such a visit would be seen as an indication that Britain, and hence the Empire, supports the Apartheid regime in South Africa....

Someone has to back down. We will see.

Australia's Prime Minister indicated that Australia will not send troops into Cambodia.

The Premier of NSW, Bob Askin, tried to make a call from a public phone. He tried three phones, and all of them were broken. He complained to the PMG, and it showed **they had been rigged** to allow a person to gather some of the coins....

They waited for the man to appear to milk the machines. He did so, and was brought before the court, and **was fined for his efforts**....

The question knowingly being **asked is if anyone less than the Premier had complained, would the phones ever have been fixed?** It is hard to believe that anyone could be so cynical, but a few people are answering in the negative.

VIETNAM WAR LOSING SUPPORT

In America, public opinion is hardening against the Vietnam war. One sign of this is that the Army will reduce the number of troops there over the next two months.

In Australia, PM Gorton has announced that the 8th Battalion will be withdrawn in a few months, and it will not be replaced. This will mean that our forces there will be reduced by 900 men, and this is a big step towards full withdrawal.

On the civilian front, there is a lot of talk about **a moratorium to the war**. This term means different things to its many supporters. At one extreme, to call a moratorium would mean that, on a certain day, all troops would pack up and go home. The war would be over, fighting would cease, and a settlement would have to be found by diplomacy.

At the other end of the range, all fighting would cease, but the troops remain in their lines, ready to resume fighting. Peace was not, at this stage, mentioned by any party.

But all of this is just civilian talk. It is among interested parties at home, wishful thinkers who have no direct influence on military thinking. So maybe it is of no avail. On the other hand, it does wear away our politicians, and maybe might move some war supporters to change their stances.

In the meantime, violence in American universities had grown even more vicious. Home Guards were being called out regularly, and these troops were lining up with bayonets fixed, and phials of tear gas, to force the protesters back.

In Australia, students were more moderate, but a "moratorium rally" was being met with **a chorus of calls for restraint that were sure to inflame the protester**s. The programme for this day included calls for all university students to sit-in all day, and for school students to boycott classes.

Comment. The Vietnam war had turned the corner. More than half the population clearly did not support it.

HOW GOOD IS OUR HEALTH SYSTEM

I reported earlier on the battles in the health industry, especially the fight over fees charged. But since then, some Letter writers have pointed out that no matter who gets the money, patients are not getting value for money, and there are all sorts of faults in the system.

I quote from just one Letter among many.

> **Letters, (Mrs) R Ruth.** Quite apart from the GPs-versus-the-Government row, our health services are and will remain a national disgrace.
>
> Hospitals are understaffed due to underpaid nurses. There is a shortage of vital equipment. Ambulances arrive at accidents with only a one-man crew. There is a huge range of drugs not in the so-called National Health Scheme (and, in the case of

the near useless sleeping pills supplied, the 50c is too much). The cost of some drugs is staggering (a certain tranquilliser at $17 per 100 tablets is hardly calculated to bring peace of mind to the paying patient). And a rapacious cardiac specialist recently quoted me $26 for an electrocardiogram.

There is no limit to this money grab. It seems the Australian public will stand for anything.

Then there is the matter of the GPs; they are scarce and overworked now yet they are greedy for more profit. It is obvious that in many cases patients have gone direct to specialists to save time and money or because their versatile local GP could not or would not do the job (I know of one suburban GP who refused to lance a boil, referring the patient to a nearby casualty department).

There are cases where a direct approach to a specialist is quite practicable despite high fees and long waiting periods; for example the annually desirable electrocardiogram for the heart (although this should be a free public service, like the chest X-ray). Then there are patients who need periodic injections for haemorrhoids or tapping of a hydrocele (both surgeon's jobs, since few GPs will do them in their non-sterile surgeries). Does the scheme mean that for all these things the patient must now trot along to the already over-crowded GP's suburban rooms for permission to proceed?

Then, in the matter of fees: just what is a GP's fee? In the old days it covered whatever you saw him for. Now the simple electric-needle removal of a wart or skin cancer is classed as a minor operation and billed accordingly at $8.

We need more GPs and specialists with fewer patients getting more thorough service under better conditions. The Government, the medical profession and the over-mild public are to blame for today's utter mess. You could die in bed tonight waiting for a doctor to come to your aid.

Comment. There were plenty of others who saw things differently. Writers compared Australia with the UK and America, and were convinced that our system was very much the better. Others compared it with the rest of the world, and there was no doubt about that.

One writer said that our system was "almost miraculous" given that our population was so small, so the infrastructure cost was shared across so few. Another pointed out that criticisms were directed at the systems, and not individuals. That meant that our doctors, nurses, specialists, and ancillary workers were doing a good job.

We could be confident that a person-to-person contact would be satisfactory, and that was considered the most important step.

A few writers found that the cost of services was good by all international comparisons. And our safety net, granted inadequate in the most extreme cases, worked well, and that meant that basic care would always be available, even to the indigent.

Second comment. At first sight, given the original complaining Letter, it seemed that our system was quite bad. But all the latter Letters painted a different picture. The conclusion was that it was pretty good.

CONCERN FOR THE QUEEN

Letters, J Holdsworth. We should, as a Commonwealth, agree to breaking Royal tradition by allowing the Queen and Duke of Edinburgh to retire from their public duties at a time or age to be determined.

Everybody else who works - and the Royals work harder than most - is entitled to the peace of retirement. Must the Queen and Duke go on working up to 18 hours a day until they die? Are they to have no rest because they have no union or employer to demand retirement?

Only Royal tradition demands this, and it is rapidly being eroded both by the Royals themselves and by the people they represent. The modern monarchy is moving with the times and getting among the people. Why should not the people themselves get with the monarchy and allow them the privilege of retirement?

Comment. 50 years after this Letter was written, the Queen is still going strong. Her son, Prince Charles, is still in waiting, and must wonder if he will ever sit on the throne.

In any case, I suggest that Queen Elizabeth is hanging in there not because she is worried about getting by on the old-age pension. I suspect that she likes the job, and would rather do that than anything else in the world. Compulsory retirement at 65 hardly seems fitting.

TRADE UNIONS UNDER SCRUTINY

The Transport Unions in NSW called strikes last Monday. That meant that there was no public transport in Sydney and most of the State. This inconvenienced millions of people, travellers, school children, employees and others, old and young.

It called attention to the lack of action that Governments were taking against the renewed epidemic of strikes that was besetting the population.

Claims were being made that Governments were in bed with the Unions, and that they would never use their own laws to enforce the orderly processes laid down by law for striking.

One writer captures many of the arguments used against strikers.

Letters, G Selby. Unionists certainly are a weird mob! They loudly claim to be striving for justice and fighting for their rights, but at the same time have not even won for themselves the elementary right of secret ballot at their own meetings.

On such a serious matter as a strike decision, they meekly suffer the ridiculous indignity of being bound by a meeting decision made by a show of hands under the critical glare of their leaders.

They demand a voice in the community so that they get a fair chance to have their views heard and their interests considered, but how often, when meeting to discuss industrial action, are they permitted a balanced presentation of both sides of the case? Where is the principle of a fair hearing when the only speakers are professional organisers whose greatest moment of glory is a headline strike?

They proudly champion the rights and freedoms of the worker, yet flatly deny a man the right to earn his living at his chosen trade unless he pays union dues which include a contribution to Labor or

Communist Party funds. There is not much right or freedom in being forced to pay fees to some political group before you can get a job.

But the weirdest anomaly of all is the malicious way unionists conduct a strike. They don't merely withhold labour in order to bring pressure to bear on an employer, they go out of their way to see that as many people suffer as possible. They attack the public at large, impoverish their mates, deprive innocent housewives and children, all with a sadistic zeal that can bring nothing but contempt and anger.

Then they proudly claim a victory against the evil bosses and expect their victims to rise from the battleground and cheer!

Personal Comment. Unionists would argue back. They would say that they had the right to strike, guaranteed by the Constitution and by State laws. They would point to the many foul and unsafe conditions that they were forced to work under. Sometimes they would claim that their pay was less than what someone else was paid.

In some cases, especially under Communist-controlled Unions, they struck for political reasons, for example, Apartheid in South Africa got them riled. There was never a shortage of reasons.

But this nation was stuck with an attitude that strikes were a normal and inevitable part of life and industrial relations. There was no thought that industrial harmony between bosses and labour could benefit both. **Ours was a shop-steward tradition, imported from the mines and factories of Britain, that demanded confrontation.**

So, strikes continued to bedevil our society, and it was only in the last 20 years that management and workers would slowly learn the benefits of mutual trust and co-operation. **Often.**

ANOTHER VIEW OF STRIKES

Letters, M Dixon. I suggest that in any future transport strike involving train and bus crews the Government should minimise public inconvenience and business loss by proclaiming the strike day a public holiday in lieu of the next statutory public holiday the State would ordinarily observe.

Thus, as soon as the Government knew there was to be a major transport hold-up on Monday it could have proclaimed the day a public holiday in lieu of the Queen's Birthday holiday on June 15.

Major sporting bodies would probably object to such a procedure but it would be up to them to adapt their programs accordingly. After all, personal and public inconvenience and business loss count more than a temporary disorganisation of sporting programs.

Comment. A worthy quote on strikes. From NSW Transport Minister, Morris. "**I am sure that if people leave their cars at home, and hitchhike to work....**"

UP TO DATE ON CRICKET NEWS

On May 22nd, the British Government approached the governing body of English cricket, and requested that it cancel the Tour by South Africa.

It appears that 14 African nations, all of them gathered into the British Empire, **have definitely decided to boycott the Commonwealth Games** if the Tour goes ahead. Several other nations outside Africa will do the same.

We will wait to see how the Government reacts.

Footnote. Our retired Prime Minister, Bob Menzies, identified as a cricket tragic, wrote that to cancel the tour would be a victory for mob rule.

REVIVING THE VERANDAH

Letters, M Earl. I would like to support Marie Knuckey in her plea for a revival of verandas. They achieve for houses what picture-hats do for women - hide the ugly and enhance the beautiful.

Sadly, as their family increases, few veranda owners can resist the temptation to close them in with handy fibro and louvres.

Let's hope a revival of interest will give the owners of such mutilated verandas the courage to strip them of their graceless additions once the children have flown the nest.

WARRANTIES ON HOUSE SALES

One Member of the NSW Legislature proposed that the sellers of existing houses provide a written guarantee to the buyer that the property meets certain requirements. Not everyone thought that this was a good thing.

Letters, Solicitor. All people who own houses, or their heirs, sooner or later will want to sell them, and they will want to be able to do so without the nightmare of facing actions for damages, which would follow in many cases as the result of such legislation.

Numerous houses would be withdrawn from sale because of the uncertainty and danger of the vendor's position. Thus the price of the remaining houses would be forced up.

The position of mortgagees selling would become most complicated and mortgage money for housing loans would become more difficult to obtain.

Comment. The idea of "Let the buyer beware" has continued to this day. But should it? Look at the number of high-rise units that are cracking and becoming uninhabitable.

SAVE THE ROO

Kangaroos have been round Australia for quite a long time. As for the rest of the world, their first thought of Australia always has some images of roos gallumphing through gum trees.

But, at a time when Aussies were getting more adventurous in their cuisine, kangaroo meat was finding its way onto the menus of a few select restaurants in the big cities. More importantly, entrepreneurs were seeing the possibilities emanating from the sale of carcases to the tables of **cities overseas**. As a consequence, our exports of roo meat were growing fast. On top of that, roo **fur** sales were in great demand overseas as, for a period, the world thought that mink stoles were not acceptable, but roo fur was.

All in all, the killing of roos was big enough to come under public scrutiny. The Letter below taps into the discussion. It stems from a remark by our Minister for Trade that **supported the expanded killing of roos** for the overseas trade.

> **Letters, D Bland.** This may be, but his attitude left much to be desired. Would it not be a greater irresponsibility to condone the virtual extinction of the red kangaroo? What may be politically

expedient or temporarily profitable may not be to any long-term advantage.

There is some merit in continuing a kangaroo meat export industry; perhaps it could have a better market potential than wool, mutton or beef (all varyingly overproduced and under-priced), but preservation and management of this resource is urgently required and vital for its continuance.

To suggest that kangaroos are a menace in general is to admit ignorance. Obviously they survived for eons before the grazing industry without turning the country into a creeping desert, as is the case due to overstocking in the semi-arid areas today.

Further, it has been shown (CSIRO) that kangaroos do not compete directly with stock for food as they prefer different species of herbage. It is the sheep and cattle which have destroyed vast areas of saltbush and mulga, not the kangaroos, yet these are the valuable fodder plants.

With about a million kangaroos slaughtered per year, this industry has a short future at its current rate of exploitation unless immediate control measures are taken.

The Australian Conservation Foundation has published recommendations in regard to the conservation of kangaroos and it is surprising not to find these recommendations heeded, particularly in view of Government grants to the Foundation to assist it in its work and preparation of such recommendations.

Comment. The trading in roo meat continued, but it never reached levels high enough for authorities to **intervene** in the overseas markets. The old joke about **eating our national emblem** might have deterred some overseas eaters, but to my taste, it was never attractive enough to encourage the eating at London prices.

JUNE NEWS ITEMS

The International Olympic Committee called for the **dropping** of soccer, alpine skiing, basketball, and ice hockey from the next Olympics.

The cricket tour of England by South Africa is still in the news. The governing body of English cricket has put the PM on then spot. **He says that the tour should be cancelled.** Well, says the MCC, if you think that, then **you should say outright that the tour is cancelled. It will then be on your political head.**

The military situation up North is getting more confused. Nixon is withdrawing some troops from Vietnam, but is pouring them into Cambodia. Congressmen are reacting "between the extremes of praise and denunciation". In other words, no one has the faintest idea of what's going on.

South Australia changed its Government to Labour, and **elected a new Premier, Don Dunstan**. Dunstan then became Australia's only Labor Premier. He was a very flamboyant character, and he was an advocate for sensible and colourful clothing for men.

Sydney University biochemist, Dr Helmyr, said that **it was possible to beat the new breathalyser** by swallowing half a pound of honey or four ounces of fructose. Fructose is a form of sugar, and not available in a pill form....

He pointed out that while it reduced the alcohol in the bloodstream, the treatment would still **impair the driver's judgement to a worse state than before....**

He added that **pills available through vending machines** at pubs and clubs provided **only one per cent** of the dose needed to reduce alcohol in the blood **to the level to deceive police**.

McLaren cars are famous among racing car enthusiasts. They are now to the forefront of **all Grand Prix. On June 2nd, Bruce McLaren was killed** on the track at Sussex in England **when his car blew up in the straight....**

Apartheid action in Victoria. South Africa sent an **official all-white football team** to play in Victoria. There was heckling of the team as the match continued**, but no action.** After the game, the South Africans huddled and then **started to sing the South African national anthem....**

This was too much for the anti-Apartheid demonstrators and wild scenes erupted. Police said that "Eight persons were arrested, several groups of persons ripped into each other. Two girls, hiding behind their skirts bit policemen, windows of the clubhouse were broken and sheds were set on fire."

Comment. International sport is often said to be the key to goodwill among nations.

GREEN BANS AND STRIKES

Back in 1950, there appeared in the Press a large number of writers who took objection to the damage being done to many different parts of the environment. Ten years ago they started to realise they would be more effective **if they formed themselves into groups and agitated in collusion together.**

By 1970, one of these groups was the **Builders' Labourers Federation**. Led by **Jack Mundy**, the Union campaigned against knocking down heritage buildings, and for creating affordable community housing, preserving green spaces, and providing safe working conditions on site.

As a Union, it had the capacity to strike at a moment's notice, to control who came and worked on building sites, and to declare "black" those building projects that it thought should not go ahead. There were many claims that it abused its power, broke the law, bullied workers and managers, and was corrupt. A number of law cases brought against it and its controllers verify that the charges were sometimes justified.

In all, the public saw the BLF as bully-boys who controlled the building of big buildings in the cities, The *SMH* editor took up the cause of the public. He pointed out that the BLF had resorted to sabotage and vandalism on sites.

He described how at the end of May, 150 members of the Union had marched miles down city streets, upsetting traffic, and this had resulted in several heated melees with police. Mundy then made a speech that said that any non-union labour used by *Master Builders Association* would be labelled a dreaded "scab", and that at the scheduled meeting next Tuesday there would be ten times as many building workers there to press the point.

He concluded, the episode was **designed to intimidate the MBA** before the next round of meetings. It was all a pattern of stand-over tactics. And the public was sick of it.

A few days later, the Editor was back. He talked about an incident in Sydney's Crows Nest where striking workers took over a construction building and caused damage in a way "that has no place in the Australian industrial scene" Then next day he talked about scuffles that broke out in Green Valley between workers and strikers. Mob lawlessness, he said, is not part of the Australian culture. In foreign countries this is common. Vigilante squads are not seen in Australia and we should all be concerned lest they become a menace to our safety and property. He finished by pointing out that Mundy was a Communist, and that he was out to make a name for himself and his Party in an extreme and adventurous manner.

Comment. This was **the beginning of a decade** of BLF intervention in all aspects of the building industry. I have pointed out the villainous side of the policy of the BLF, and if it **seems** bad, it **was** indeed bad. It wasted any resources you could think of, it bankrupted businesses, and corrupted men and corporations.

But despite the tactics it used, or whatever the motives of Mundy and his colleagues, it did have **the effect** of slowing down the rapacious speed at which corporations and others were changing the face of the nation. And it did have **the effect** of saving the lives and limbs of countless workers. And it did have **the effect** of preserving green spaces that would otherwise have been lost to the cities. **Whatever conservationists in Australia currently achieve, they are building on the legacy of Jack Mundy.**

Letters, J Healy. You refer to "Australia's enviable tradition of non-violence in strikes." Unfortunately, this is not the tradition. The following industrial disputes all had force and violence:

The miners' dispute at Ballarat in December, 1854.

The shearers' dispute in 1891, when they were confronted in the Clermont area by 200 police reinforced by artillerymen and mounted infantry, with weapons including a machine-gun and a field-piece.

The waterside dispute in November, 1928, when police in Melbourne fired into a group of demonstrating workers, wounding four.

In December, 1929, police armed with rifles fired on striking miners at Rothbury, wounding seven and killing one.

These are only some examples; and they do not include house raids on active unionists and arrests and imprisonment over the years.

Letters, W Lakeman. In 1800 trade-unions were illegal. Over the years they have won certain rights: the right to bargain collectively to better members' conditions; the right to strike; the right to picket. Very few of us would deny them these hard-won rights.

One right they have not won, however, is the right to destroy other people's property. If an ordinary person damages the property of another he is compelled to pay compensation. Why should not the builders' labourers union be forced to make good destruction caused by its members? If the union has insufficient funds a levy on its members could supply them.

Whatever is done to settle the present dispute - and let us hope it is soon - we must not tolerate vandalism or stand-over tactics.

THE CRICKET TOUR BY SOUTH AFRICA

The British Government was faced with a difficult question. **On the one hand**, the Tour was being organised by a private body that owed nothing to any other body, and certainly not to any political Party.

On the other hand, it was clear that if the Tour went ahead, public safety would be in danger because the opponents were organising protests at the grounds, and these were certain to get out of hand, and lead to punch-ups and even riots. And if it went ahead, most of the black teams to the Games would not attend.

The British Prime Minister, Harold Wilson, finally cancelled the Tour. His Labour Government was of course bashed by the Tories, but was also criticised by his own Labour Party. How could he, they asked, capitulate to the mob who were threatening violence and at the same time, set a precedent that the nation would come to regret?

Wilson's decision opened up all sorts of questions. What if an **all-black** team from New Zealand wanted to visit? The Harlem Globe Trotters at that time were all black. Would they be banned? The organisers of the opposition to the Tour were threatening to block similar tours from other nations in future. How long would the Government wait until it took action against the group?

Here in Australia, the mood was mixed. I told you earlier that Bob Menzies thought that mob law had triumphed. But others thought differently.

Letters, J Patch. May a visiting Englishman suggest that Sir Robert Menzies should retire to his rocking chair in the afternoon light?

As an ex-Prime Minister he is showing a lack of manners in commenting on something that does not concern him, i.e. the British Government's request to the Cricket Council to cancel the South African cricket tour. As a private individual he shows a lack of appreciation of what is happening in the world today.

I am not a long-haired rebel nor a woolly minded academic. Indeed, I am a Conservative voter who will vote against Mr Wilson in the coming election. But faced with the stubborn disregard of the Cricket Council for matters outside cricket, the Labour Government had no option but to intervene.

For people in Britain, South Africa and in this country to talk of the British Government introducing politics into sport is to ignore that it was South Africa which did exactly that and is arrogantly challenging about it.

To reverse the situation, I wonder what those who talk of blackmail would say if a South African became world featherweight boxing champion and Lionel Rose were prevented from going there to challenge him.

Letters, J McHarg. For 30-odd years I have been a supporter of Sir Robert Menzies, in good times and bad, and have occasionally taken up the cudgels on his behalf in your columns. It is sad to find myself now in the opposite camp on the South African cricket tour issue.

While we all deplore the lawlessness and excesses threatened, and while conceding that a possibly dangerous precedent has been created, surely the blame for the whole affair rests squarely on the Cricket Council? In the present climate it was wrong to invite the South Africans, and the wrong was perpetuated as time went on, leaving the British Government no option than to intervene.

As you say [in editorial], it is South Africa which has brought politics into sport. If they wish to persevere with their inhuman policies they must be prepared to accept the role of outcasts. We should not encourage them by inviting their all-white teams when they persist in dictating whom other nations should send to their country.

There is some recent evidence that the lesson may be getting home - if it is not, the South Africans can enjoy an all-white series with their Rhodesian friends and neighbours. It would not provide much of a cricket spectacle, but would have the great virtue of being racially spotless.

Comment. This battle with South Africa over **its Apartheid policy** went on for over a decade more. Most Governments in the world opposed it, but were not prepared to imposed tariffs against South Africa because it would hurt **their own** trade. But they could apply pressure through their sporting teams and their tours. So, in effect, South Africa was barred from international sport for a dozen more years. When tours did go ahead, **all those concerned were harassed by organised groups**, and the tours were disappointments, and not the triumphs for sport as they were intended.

OLDIES NOT SO WELL OFF

There were many retired and elderly people in the nation who were poor. Many others who were doing a bit better, but were by no means wealthy. Some had pensions, some had super, some had the dole equivalent, some had nothing but their wits.

So there were plenty of Letters complaining about how hard it was to enjoy life.

Letters, D Munro. Close on 70 years ago when I was a small nipper in Scotland my dad told me that the Highlanders never died and that every five years a detachment of Gordon Highlanders were sent up to shoot the oldest ones. In my youthful innocence I believed him.

The memory of that spoof prompts me to ask why all the fuss about the "unwanteds," sometimes known as senior citizens or pensioners? Of what use are they? They served their day and generation and helped to build the country we live in, which apparently is not to their credit as it finds itself unable to support them decently now they are of no use to it.

Everywhere the cry is for more money, the only beneficiary being the Federal Treasury. But as the wages go up so does the cost of living, reducing the "unwanteds" to an even lower existence.

We claim to be a Christian community taught to "honour thy father and mother." One of the attributes of the Christian is kindness, so how about inquiring if there are any unused or surplus gas chambers left over in Germany from the last war? The use of them would be demonstrating by painless extermination, kindness instead of indifference to the slow starvation which is the lot of so many of the "oldies." They are a section of our community with no strike weapon to fight for a better deal.

The unions are very active in their endeavours to secure better wages and conditions for their members but forget those same members are the "unwanteds" of tomorrow and apparently lose interest in them then. I cannot recall any industrial action to improve the lot of the pensioners.

I've given one suggestion, has Mr Gorton a better?

Letters, Widow. Mr T Ramster wants more money for himself and the other 14,000 superannuants under the State Superannuation Act and I wish him and his colleagues well.

But what of my husband and the scores of thousands of other temporary Public servants who are retired after many years of loyal and continuous service with no superannuation at all?

It is to the eternal discredit of Labor that they permitted this iniquitous temporary system to continue during their 25 years in office and it is no feather in the cap of the Askin Government that the system survives to this day.

At the last State election Mr Askin did make a solemn pledge that he would introduce a superannuation scheme for temporary

Public servants, but it is a pledge the Premier will never keep as far as my husband is concerned, for he was retired late last year and died two months ago.

Personal comment. Every writer had his own complaints and most of them had some semblance of a suggested solution. But there was no easy solution. As money became available, some of these complaints were fixed. Then a few years later, some different ones. Gradually, the social services for the elderly improved until we reach the situation that we are in today.

I do not want to be trampled underfoot by writers telling of their **current** grievances, so I hasten to say **there is still plenty to grizzle at. And still some people who are barely surviving**.

But when I compare the situation to that of 1970, **the bulk of the aged population now is ever so much better off than they were then**.

MERCY KILLINGS

An Adelaide Church of England Minister argued that Australian society should be prepared to discuss **the mercy killing of brain defective infants and children, and also the old and infirm**. He was not rich in detail, and had no advice on how to implement such killings. He simply said that it was time the nation faced up to the discussion. He added as an aside that he expected to be criticised by the Catholic Church, which was the main advocate against such killings.

The gentleman below took an opposite point of view.

Letters, (Rev Bro) Benedict. Professor Welford is not telling us anything new when he says society will have to decide if it is right to keep alive senile people and mentally defective infants.

After all, wasn't the precedent set 30 years ago in Germany's National Socialist State? Does Professor Welford visualise extermination centres similar to Hitler's?

He specifically mentions the mercy killing of senile people and mentally defective children. On this point I take issue with him.

In nursing the senile and training retarded children over the past 20 years I have not once come across a single case of one wanting to be "put to sleep." On the contrary, the senile have a tenacious hold on life, and the retarded love every minute of it. What sort of Christian minister is this who would abolish God's Commandment: "Thou shalt not kill"?

Professor Welford guessed rightly that violent opposition would arise "particularly from the Roman Catholic Church." Is this the only institution unanimous in its stand for the sacredness of human life?

I am often asked why the Catholic Church conducts hospitals and homes for retarded children. It is often pointed out - and quite rightly too - that the State can conduct such institutions efficiently and well. There are many answers to this question, but here is the obvious one: "To be a refuge from those who advocate ridding society of an unwanted burden."

I might add, too, that the Church takes very seriously Christ's words: "Whatsoever you shall do to these the least of my little ones, you shall do unto me." (Matthew XI.29,30).

Then another popped up and hoped to winnow some of the chaff from the grain.

Letters, R Watters. Every time a clergyman cannot find an argument to support his position, he lapses back on quoting the Bible. O'Grady does this twice, and thus dodges the issue.

I can think of a dozen arguments as to why and when forms of euthanasia might be used to terminate life. And I can think of a dozen arguments against using them.

And I can think of a dozen arguments from the Bible that might be construed to pass judgement on such matters.

But to ignore these and simply quote silly random bits from the Bible is dereliction of duty.

Comment. I agree with R Watters that there are multiple arguments for and against euthanasia and have no intention of presenting them to you.

I will simply say that about 50 years later, around 2020, the matter is still before the public, and at last people are facing up to the problem.

For example, Victoria in 2019 passed legislation that allowed "voluntary assisted dying" to its residents. Other States are mulling it, and it appears that some others will actually adopt euthanasia when a few stay-put politicians are removed from the various State Houses of Parliament.

But it has taken 50 years to get even to that stage.

HOPES FOR A BETTER WORLD

The NSW Labor Party have decided to **introduce a 35-hour-week as soon as possible** to replace the current 40-hours. The move will meet with opposition from employers, but the Labor Party thinks **the economy can stand the extra strain.**

JULY NEWS ITEMS

The "revised" National Health scheme started on July 1st. The scene is very confused. For example, the fee for a GP consultation is now pitched at the average fee **previously** charged. And this has now been prescribed as the **minimum** fee to be charged. But some doctors who charged **less** than the average **will now have to raise their prices** to meet the new requirements. Someone has to pay for this, and it is not quite certain who....

An information booklet was supposed to be ready for the population by July 1st. But, due to delays in decision-making it will be two months late....

And many more immediate complaints. Still, it is a huge task ahead, and it could well settle down to something better that the current scheme. **Give them a go.**

Newington is a Methodist GPS school in Sydney that attracts some of the most prominent families in the State of NSW. **Any public statement by its Headmaster attracts much attention**....

The Head master was dismissed by the School Council because he advocated that **young men defy the National Service Act which conscripts young men to** serve in Vietnam....

50 Methodist clergy and 50 prominent laymen have signed an open Letter **demanding that he not be sacked.**

In Bellbird, a NSW country town, **two brothers started laughing cynically when the charges against a relative were read out**. They continued to do so after being directed to stop. Finally, the judge sentenced them for contempt of Court, and **gaoled them for 24 hours.**

In Melbourne, a man killed a woman and her four children, and put their bodies into a car. This was driven to a nearby sea-side cliff and pushed into the ocean. But **it came to rest on a ledge, on all four wheels,** and was not devoured by the ocean as expected. Police are questioning the husband.

A Committee of the Methodist Conference of NSW **decided by 41 - 33 votes not to sack the Headmaster**.

The Prime Minister, John Gorton, has **refused a request for a referendum** by the Island of Bougainville to enable it to secede from Papua-New Guinea. This island is rich in copper, and development by Rio Tinto is happening. **The natives are reluctant to share their new wealth with all New Guinea.** Hence their wish for secession....

This is an important issue for the people of Bouganville, and for Rio Tinto, and will grow into a series of major problems.

SIR WILLIAM YEO'S DELIGHT

Returned servicemen from WWI and WWII had, over the years, organised themselves into various associations to protect their rights and sought the benefits promised to them when they signed up for service. By 1970, their main representative body was the Returned Servicemens League, and one of the popular offshoots of this was **a number of licensed Clubs** in all large population centres around Australia.

The Chairman of this RSL group was Sir William Yeo. He had come to the point where he was often criticised for his extreme right-wing views. He had an opinion on all things connected to the military, past and present and future, and voiced these in emphatic and aggressive terms. Sometimes he reflected the views of his membership, sometimes he was well wide of the mark.

He had been to Paris recently, and had witnessed the marches there against the Vietnam War. He, of course, supported the War, and took some delight in the fact that the police and military were quite prepared to rough up the tumultuous elements rioting there.

He reported that "Gendarmes, finding demonstrators lying in the streets, simply dragged them over the cobblestones to police trucks. Girls were dragged by their hair. To clear the area, fire-hoses were turned on demonstrators. **It was the loveliest thing I have seen in my life.**"

Comment. There was a large number of people who would have supported him. There were always comments here about our own police being **too tolerant** of thugs who mixed with genuine demonstrators simply for the thrill of the violence they could generate.

CONCERN OVER NEW POLLUTIONS

The Letter below, from an American friend, is one of many that were starting to find their way into Letters columns. There were lots of Letters about environmental issues, and pollution of land and water. But this is **one of the earliest about pollution of the air and the atmosphere.**

> **Letters, D Romano.** I had the good fortune to live and work in Sydney from 1960 to 1965 as managing director of an American firm's Australian subsidiary. At the time I was firmly convinced that Sydney was the world's most beautiful city, favoured as it was by a natural harbour and lovely beaches second to none.
>
> I have just returned with my family to settle in Australia. The Harbour and the beaches are still there, but whatever has happened to the beautiful clean air that was once every Sydneyite's birthright?
>
> As I write, I am in a flat in Mosman with a panoramic view of the city stretching from the Harbour Bridge to Vaucluse. The entire scene is covered with a murky brown, disgusting layer of industrial waste

reaching to the top of the Australia Square building and partially blocking the view of its lower floors. Clouds of thick brown smoke are billowing upwind of the city and spreading out to sea on the offshore breeze.

It is bad enough to look at this filthy blanket. It is even worse to think that I will shortly join several hundred thousand other hapless souls who must spend all or part of the day working or shopping under these conditions.

I will contribute time, money and any other energies I have to stopping this insidious and unnecessary poisoning of the air we breathe.

I have watched this tragedy enacted for five years during my recent stay in the United States.

I say "no" to such a fate for Sydney; and I say we, you and I, have it in our power to stop the present trend before it's too late.

In the few minutes it has taken to write this, my view of the Eastern suburbs has been obliterated.

All that is visible now is the tip of Australia Square and the vague outline of some tall buildings in Darling Point. The rest is totally blotted out, covered in smoke...

Twenty-four hours later, I find the wind has shifted around from offshore to onshore; once again our lovely city lies gleaming like a jewel among the blue waters of the bay.

The conclusion is obvious: the culprits responsible for yesterday's filthy air are one or more industries lying inland of the city, perhaps in the near western suburbs. When the wind is from the ocean their noxious gases are blown inland, leaving the city clean and sparkling (small consolation for those living to the west). When the breeze is offshore, however, an entire city of two million people is covered in murk.

Rather than depend on the bounty of nature to provide an onshore breeze so that we can breathe clean air, why not determine which industries are at fault and correct the problem at its source?

It's not hard, but it takes time and costs money. And that's what good local government is all about, spending the time and the money to guarantee that the precious resources of all are not abused by a few.

Comment. Mr Romano was right when he said that some of the pollution came and went with the winds, But there was also much coming from within the cities. Take Sydney as an example. Bunnerong Power Station day after day, year after year, belched huge black clouds of smoke into the air. It was about five miles from the centre of Sydney, and no matter where the wind came from, someone had to live under its spell.

Local opposition to this pollution was one of the reasons that it closed by 1975. The same was true in other cities around the nation. **By 1970, the population was becoming aware** of the dangers to our clear blue skies, and the health impact that followed from putting our industrial waste into the atmosphere.

But as another example of how that attitude of ordinary people was changing, I present this Letter on noise pollution. Such a Letter would not have been thought of even five years previously.

Letters, P Benson. It is refreshing indeed to read an airline pilot's view of noise abatement procedures at Sydney airport.

He can be well assured that the preferred runway system operating after 7pm at night is greatly appreciated by many residents of the St George district.

It should be noted that these procedures came into operation shortly after evidence by the Rockdale citizens' noise committee had been submitted to the Select Parliamentary Committee on aircraft noise.

As to his statement that these procedures add at least 8 per cent airborne time to his schedules on a domestic airline this slight delay is insignificant compared with the sudden blatant intrusion of jet aircraft on an otherwise quiet community.

The delay probably could be reduced further if the airline companies did away with the ridiculous parallel timetable system which results in a large proportion of two airlines' entire fleet attempting to land and take off simultaneously.

His final statement, "if all international airports observed a curfew similar to Sydney's it would take a Qantas 707 in excess of three days to reach London," does not take into consideration that the locations of airports en route, in relation to community environment, are very different from that of Sydney's Kingsford Smith Airport.

Comment. Do not worry about the details of runways and so on. Just note that **noise has been added to the list of environmental matters** that an increasingly aware society was just starting to become anxious about. And about the counter arguments about the longer duration of flights. As usual, there are many sides to every issue.

THE NEWINGTON SCHOOL MATTER

The trouble at Newington School brought forth many Letters that focused on whether or not our troops should be in Vietnam. These arguments had been well worn by now, and a **school** issue was unlikely to move people out of their entrenched positions.

But a number of Letters did attack the central issue. The first one quoted here defended the Headrnaster.

> **Letters, A Lawes.** As an Old Newingtonian of some years standing and one who has always maintained a continuing interest in the school I dissociate myself completely from the actions both of the College Council and the Council of the Old Newingtonians Union in seeking to dismiss the Headmaster, the Rev D Trathen.
>
> I believe these actions have done great harm to the school and have not the approval of very many Old Boys.
>
> The College Council has specifically recognised Mr Trathen's sincerity and academic qualifications, but nevertheless has sought to silence him because his views were not acceptable to it. If this principle is accepted by the community, no one answerable to a council or to a board of directors has much personal freedom left; educationists in particular could see before them the ugly alternatives of silence and conformity, or dismissal.

Even more important, though, than the civil rights aspect of the matter is the reason for Mr Trathen's stand, namely the immoral war in Vietnam and the unjust National Service Act. No Christian can accept the law as his final standard of conduct in all matters, and the Nuremburg trials established the principle that in matters of grave human concern the ultimate responsibility rests squarely on the individual, notwithstanding laws which may be in force at the time or the orders of a superior. Clearly Mr Trathen is on solid ground on both counts and talk of anarchy in such circumstances is plain nonsense.

The second one did not.

Letters, P Pym. The Headmaster is in the employ of a school. He is there to implement the policy of the school. If his own would-be policy conflicts with that of the school, no one could argue that **his** policy should dominate. In such a situation, he must abandon his own preferences, and either shut up or leave,

That is exactly the situation at Newington now. He is at loggerheads with the School, and those are the two options that he has.

There is no point in saying that he can continue to oppose the Law School **in a**

private capacity. As soon as he accepted the role of Headmaster, he became an official spokesman for the School. **Nothing he says now can be seen as private.** After he leaves his home in the morning, he is on display as a representative of the School. He should remember that, and if he still pronounces alternative views, then he should not wait to be sacked. **He should pack up and go.**

Comment. As you read in News Items, he did not pack up. He was retained by the School. But, in fact, he did not return again to this fray in public.

RIGHT TO PROTEST

The proposed legislation to curb violence in protest marches contains various penalties and also a requirement that demonstrations can be held only with the permission on the Police Commissioner.

Remember that this is not the normal state of affairs. People in this nation, in normal times, do not care much about behaviour in demonstrations because there are none to worry about. It is only because of the Vietnam war that marchers and mobs are gathering with a common voice of protest.

The Police Commissioner comes into the matter especially with the marches. He has a legitimate role there because any decent-sized march means such things as traffic disruption, street closures, and paddy wagons to take away any stirrers.

Different views emerged on the Commissioner's role.

Letters, J McCurrich. In my innocence I have always believed we fought two world wars and are currently in Vietnam to preserve democracy. This democracy covers the right to protest and lawfully demonstrate against matters with which we do not agree.

Over the years, partly as a result of increasing density of population, it has been necessary to limit the freedom of the individual. However, each restriction must be considered with great care.

The proposals now before State Cabinet transgress all reason and concepts of democracy. I do not disagree with harsher penalties for vandalism; in fact I support them, but the discretionary and arbitrary powers conferred by the proposed indictable offence deemed an "aggravating offence", and the requirement that all demonstrations must be licensed, are abhorrent and must be strongly opposed by all thinking individuals.

Should a Police Commissioner be given the right to determine the topics on which an individual may protest?

Never!

Letters, ATH. We cannot have a city where people decide to have a march, and then get others to join, and then march down the street shouting and playing their guitars and singing Red anthems. Every day we would have disruption of traffic, accidents, and fights with spectators. It would be bedlam, chaos.

Marches have to be planned, organised, scheduled, so that controls can be put into place. This is only partially for the benefit of the marchers, but mainly for the bulk of the population who want an orderly way of going about their business.

So, there has to be a person who adds up any competing demands, and then says a march may or may not go ahead. The most likely person is the Police Commissioner. Give him the job, and trust him.

Comment. The above writers were both missing the point. The demos were breaking into violence because they were being infiltrated by a minority whose sole purpose was to disrupt the parade. If they got a punch or two in the head, they were heroes. If they got fined, it was only a few bob that some well-meaning better-off donor paid. Both sides of the argument did this. And both men and women were in those disruptive minorities.

SYDNEY'S SECOND AIRPORT

The air traffic into Sydney was already big enough to encourage people and interested parties to talk quite definitely about a second airport. Most of the proposals were based on bread-and-butter mundane ideas that blatantly pushed some particular interest.

But this one below, has a bit of flair.

Letters, C Sorenson. The possible location of Sydney's second airport some miles off-shore does not appear to have been considered by the authorities despite the fact that the engineering practicability of such construction has been demonstrated in a number of studies.

The recent report by British Public Building and Works, examines the possibilities of building various forms of off-shore airports.

It states that the siting of future airports at sea is perhaps the only way of dealing with the problem of aircraft noise.

Of the various types examined in the report the most practicable for Sydney would appear to be a platform supported by piles or caissons and connected to the land by a rapid-transit system using tunnels or bridges augmented perhaps by hovercraft, hydrofoils, and aircraft that are less noisy than the big jets.

A feasibility study, not yet completed, is being made for a new three-deck international airport for Los Angeles located 10 miles at sea in approximately 240ft of water and connected with the shore by a tunnel.

Another similar huge airport five miles from land has been proposed for New York. The opportunity to dispose readily of the city's treated garbage and sewage into the ocean is another advantage which could accrue from the construction of such a platform. The costs of such structures could be high, but these could be largely offset by the value of the land which could be released for other purposes and the tremendous intangible advantage of having noise-free skies.

Comment. The authorities had a fair bit of time to think about this. **About fifty years in fact**. It was only in 2018 that a site was announced. And that, alas for Mr Sorenson, was not out to sea, but 30 miles inland from Sydney.

KILLARA HIGH SCHOOL

A parent of three children, attending a major Sydney public High School, pointed out that several of the amenities of the school were not available because of building that was going on there.

She pointed out that some children had to walk up to 50 yards to go to the toilet. That they might have to wait up to five minutes to collect their salads from the tuck shop, now called a canteen. That heating was available only during class time and not available to heat the rooms pre-class. That there was a draft in one classroom coming in from a window that was patched only with several sheets of cardboard. And all of this would go on for the full week, she feared.

Comment. I am not a grump who hates children. I don't care much whether they are too soft, or too spoilt. And I want them to have conditions better than those above. But I can remember going to school **every** day, thirty years earlier, under tougher conditions than those just mentioned. And I bet that some readers could make your hair stand on end with their own tales of doing the same, and the quality of buildings and amenities. Especially in the country, whether it be in towns, or country cities.

I won't dwell on this. I will just add that no one at my schools **ever** complained about having inadequate heating. **Can you guess why?**

AUGUST NEWS ITEMS

A plane high-jacking in America has set a record. A Boeing 747 scheduled to go to Puerto Rico was forced to land in Cuba, It had **a massive 379 passengers on board....**

A novel twist was that **the high-jacker left the plane in Havana** and the plane was then able to continue to its original destination. The villain, with his gun, was arrested.

Good news and bad news from **the egg industry. The price of eggs will officially drop** by 5 cents a dozen to 56 cents for large eggs. But the Commonwealth's **egg levy of One Dollar per hen per year** will remain.

Most of the industry claim they cannot pay this....

This is a reminder that **Government regulations**, of quite small matters, **were still (post war) loitering** and frustrating business and persons.

A new service has started in Sydney. A 24-hour **pollution alarm system** will accept telephone calls, and they will be investigated. Cases of backyard burning will be referred to Councils, and it will not accept calls about motor vehicles or smoking on buses....

There were 110 calls on the first day.

Chemists in NSW will be able to open 15 hours a day, instead of the present 10.

Danger signs for the nickel boom. Nickel Mines of Australia reported that a promising site had in fact **no commercial deposits**. Its shares fell from $30 to $5 in a day.

Cowra defeated Bathurst Charlestons **110 - 4** in a Rugby League match at Bathurst over the week-end.

Famous Australian marathon swimmer, **Des Renford, swam from Dover in England to France,** across the English Channel, in 13 hours, 9 minutes. He had 10 minutes rest, and then **started to swim back to the start**....

Five miles from Dover, his escort boat ran into him in high seas. **It broke his shoulder.** He was pulled from the water, and **so his attempt at the double record was foiled**.

A rare Galapagos Island tortoise is in a serious condition at Sydney's Taronga Zoo after vandals threw rocks at her and **broke her shell.**

The respected British magazine, **the New Scientist,** estimates that **Australia could build 36 20-kilotonne atom bombs a year** after the Jervis Bay reactor has been built....

That Jervis Bay reactor was never built, so we were denied the pleasure of stockpiling atom bombs. A quick bit of arithmetic suggests that we **could have had about 1,000 by now. That would surely make us all feel safer.**

BANKERS NEED A REST, MUST BE AUGUST

Letters, J Hearne. How much longer does the majority of the general public have to be inconvenienced by the outmoded and archaic custom known as Bank Holiday?

Because the banks observe this sacred day, the stock exchange and many businesses associated with finance also do not open. But why should State Government departments, local councils and others also jump on the bandwaggon?

This fact was brought to my attention on Monday of this week, when I found the Baby Health Centre in my district was closed because of the "public" holiday. I felt this was particularly annoying, as we are only provided with this "service" in our area on one day of the week. I had gone to the centre on the previous Thursday, when it is normally open, to find a notice on the door, authorised by Hornsby Council, which subsidises the clinic, stating that the centre was closed for that day but would be open as usual on Monday August 3. However by Monday someone had remembered that it was Bank Holiday and the date on the notice had been changed. I wonder how many other young mothers in NSW had been inconvenienced in a similar manner due to the closing of one section of one Government department.

It seems to me that Bank Holiday is a useless, out-of-date custom practised by banks and other bodies and institutions which are already giving a limited service to the public. It is high time the State Government legislated to abolish an unnecessary holiday which gives leisure to a few, at the expense and inconvenience of very many.

Comment. We all know that bankers need a rest. So it is nice to see that in 1970 the quaint idea that a holiday, the first Monday in August, should be set aside to give them a break. And it is nice to see that anyone vaguely associated with finance could also take the day off.

But of course, by 2020, this old-world custom has now gone, and the bankers and related financial houses, and Baby Care Clinics, now work the same days as the rest of us.

Or, do they?

URBAN SPRAWL

All our major cities were growing fast. And that meant that many outer suburbs, previously out in the bush on the edges of civilisation, were now being built out by the growth of the middle class. This brought nice things like sealed roads and pavements, and sewers, and garbage services every week. Perhaps also, bus services. But it **also** created problems.

Letters, H Scott. When Mr Askin and his Cabinet are setting out the pattern of the proposed legislation concerning pollution for the parliamentary draftsmen to follow it might be as well for them to give serious thought to the effect which legal precedent has on this problem.

For over a hundred years our Courts have invariably followed the rule that because a person or company established a factory (perhaps a small one) out in what was once thick bush country on the outskirts of Sydney they have a right to continue their operations no matter how many homes are built around those factories.

The factory, say our Courts, was there first and people should not build their homes nearby if they cannot tolerate the smells and noises and other hazards generated by industry. So land-hungry people are forced by the Courts to put up with hazards which in fact the Courts should protect them from.

There are factories generating rotten egg smells continuously in the centre of areas of beautiful homes. There are factories generating noises you would never hear if you lived near a steelworks. Language shouted by employees of these factories is really flowery, radios blare all day long and powdery dust gets everywhere.

Some of these are what aldermen call backyard factories and heaven knows Sydney has more than its share of them all protected by an obsolete legal precedent which is upheld by most health inspectors of local councils despite the fact that the hazards are such as to place them well within the confines of their duties as guardians of public health.

If the Askin Government really wants to put teeth into its legislation against pollution it should ask Mr Maddison to abolish this precedent and, while he is at it, ask Mr Morton to give local councils power to send such factories out to new pastures of tick country.

Comment. This was a problem that has never been solved completely. If you look round many of the old suburbs in the cities even today, you can find small areas of factories and warehouses stuck inconspicuously among the older tile and brick cottages. I suppose gradually they are being weeded out, but the process has been so very slow.

THE FUNERAL INDUSTRY

The funeral industry was making headlines. **Firstly**, because of the advent of big money into the old industry. **Family units** were being bought out, and corporate objectives and consolidation were taking their place.

Secondly, changes such as those mooted below were having an effect.

> **Letters, WB.** Anyone on the side of life and the living must be concerned at the recent growth of the funeral industry - or more accurately, the death industry.
>
> This industry is now employing door-to-door salesmen and, by means of skillful publicity, is endeavouring to glamorise death. Memorial parks and lawn cemeteries are springing up around Sydney and the notion is being fostered that we should accept funerals US-style, with expensive plots, grotesque rigmarole and fractured bank accounts. This is one aspect of American progress we can well do without.
>
> Death may be the end for the deceased, but it is often the beginning of a very heavy debt burden for the survivors. Surely in this age we should be able to make our exit in simple dignity without the needless fuss and extravagance recommended by the death industry.

Death was a subject that was scarcely talked about. Likewise, funeral arrangements were not common topics of conversation around the Sunday barbie.

Average people had not reached such a level of affluence that funeral costs could be easily absorbed. The end result of this was that most people opted for a just-above-the-minimum cost approach, and saw the Americanisation of funerals as something to be avoided.

But, as usual, someone disagreed. And his selling spiel was a bit higher-minded than most people at the time were prepared to accept.

Letters, R Taffs, Managing Director, Pine Grove Memorial Park Limited. The comments of WB regarding the funeral industry are typical of the uninformed. He is quite prepared to be critical of an industry of which he obviously has little knowledge.

His comments regarding American-style services are utterly ridiculous. Because the Press and other media have from time to time suggested that the memorial parks and lawn cemetery development in Australia follows an American concept, he immediately accepts this as a truth.

The concept of lawn cemeteries originated in England and Europe - not for purposes of flamboyancy, rigmarole, or glamorising - but an effort to eradicate the disgraceful neglect evident in monumental type cemeteries.

The strongest case that can be presented for memorial parks and lawn cemeteries is the introduction of a permanent maintenance fee which is incorporated as a cost factor in all services rendered. This fee is lodged in trust, the capital of which can never be dissipated, but the income earned will be used for future maintenance. Neglect will never be evident in this new concept of cemeteries or crematoriums.

Modern cemetery administrators, many of whom are specialists, in engineering, landscaping or business administration, believe that cemeteries should do more than honour the departed. Since they are part of the history and culture of every Australian community, they also should encourage visitation of the living by the development of a parklike atmosphere.

Modern cemeteries and the funeral industry in general are concerned with the problem of the living and how best to serve their families. The funeral service is of a few hours' duration, but the cemetery has an everlasting obligation. Reverence for the resting place of those who have gone before us, has been part of our history from the dawn of time. Memorials may change over the years, but the purpose behind them never has and never will.

Finally, the concept of pre-arrangement is like medical benefits and other family protection services. It gives the opportunity to acquire the services a family will require at today's cost and solves a problem that can be most painful and as WB observes "the beginning of a very heavy debt burden for the survivors."

The choice can be with dignity and without extravagance when pre-arranged, because it can be discussed logically. It is only when emotion takes over that irrational arrangements are made.

Comment. Let me rave for a minute. This was also a time when existing monumental cemeteries were under constant attack from Letter-writers because they were overgrown and generally neglected. People were still sentimental and loving about the deceased, but these neglected cemeteries bore testimony to a general feeling that the here-and-now was all important.

You could see it in attendances at Anzac Day marches. You could see it when youth flocked to glitzy American pop performances and not to symphonies. Large sections of the community, the Baby Boomers, just wanted to get on with life, perhaps make a fortune, and forget the symbols of the past. Forget religion, and all the restraints that it carried with it. And as for Mum when she died, there was no point in spending big money on her funeral. The kids needed it more.

Second comment. The above comment might sound critical of the Boomers. Perhaps it is, a bit. But there is a lot of sense in every part of it. It's just like real life. It ain't black and white.

REVENUE FROM PEDESTRIANS

Letters, P Butler. With ever-increasing traffic densities, the forecast of perhaps twice this density within two decade and lamentably little road-building in the interim, surely consideration must be given to the testing and licensing of all road users other than drivers and cyclists; namely the pedestrians.

Every year the people become more and more the target for accidents. Few have learned the increased dangers of crossing vehicle paths since the days when it was quite common in the country to stop virtually in the middle of the street for a chat. The speed of wheeled movement has increased to a degree that such an act in a city street would be tantamount to suicide.

Daily, pedestrians move across the street oblivious to the dangers - and how often these people, particularly the young and the infirm, are struck down, often fatally!

A system of instruction, testing and licensing might limit the number of pedestrians breaking the law, and some visible recording number could assist in police apprehension of the more agile. Stiff penalties as well as an annual registration fee could be further stimuli in the improvement of pedestrian behaviour.

A few writers were quick to support this "splendid" idea.

Letters, H Bullock, Pedestrian. Mr Butler's plea for licensing pedestrians is interesting. The main problem in implementing it will be that every pedestrian must have a numberplate.

Where will it be affixed?

One solution is to have small sandwich boards hung over the shoulders but a question remains. Men will have no trouble, neither will the willowy woman. But what to do with the ample bosom which will give such a tilt to the plate that the constabulary may have difficulty reading it?

Perhaps we could have our numbers woven into the front and back of our outer clothing. This would have major economic significance as we could not use others' cast-offs, and the new styles which would evolve from this novelty would ensure a major boom in the clothing industry.

Thanks to Mr Butler for a very entertaining idea. I shall await his appearance on Sydney's streets sporting his "L" plate with much interest.

Another person wrote that **annual** licensing of pedestrians would be good, and that **persons should be tested first** before getting a licence to walk. Another suggested that meters could be worn by all pedestrians, and the charges be based on how far they walked each month.

Another wanted an exemption if a woman was pushing a pram, though she would have to prove that the pram was occupied by a baby before she could get the exemption.

Councils, though, have been slow to adopt any of these ideas. It could be that there were practical difficulties in the fool-proof collection of revenue. Although, in this age of the 2020's, when talk about Artificial Intelligence is rife, it may be possible to re-think.

THANKS TO THE UNIONS

Communists inside this nation were fighting a rear-guard action to disrupt the economy to the point where it would collapse. Foolish as it seems, some Red-led Trade Unions were still hoping that somehow they could bring about a glorious revolution that would sweep away capitalism and replace it with the wonders of the Soviet Union.

Thus, these Unions were intent on disrupting any of the normal functions of government. The one weapon they could legally use was the strike, and as we have seen earlier, they used it prodigiously.

The results showed up all over the place. Below is a neat Letter from a soldier whose luxuries were reduced by one of the multitude of strikes imposed willy nilly by the Reds.

Letters, The Soldiers in Vietnam. The members of the Australian Forces serving in Vietnam wish to convey to the leaders and members of the Unions in Australia now on strike, our greatest admiration in the way they are stopping our mail both in and out of Australia because of the fuel shortage.

Also we now find our R and R to Australia has been suspended because of them. Can we point out that we only see our families and loved ones for six days out of 12 months and we are even denied this small luxury which we really look forward to.

A NEW GUINEA UNSOLVED PROBLEM

To end this Chapter, I include a Letter from another world, in another time.

Letters, R Gyles. I shall restrict myself to his statements concerning land tenure by indigenes. He contends that no Papuan or New Guinea native has ever owned land. Using the word "owned" in our sense that may be correct.

There can be no doubt, however, that by native custom, groups of indigenes at the time of European occupation had traditional areas of land in which the group communally exercised rights of use and occupation to the exclusion of other groups of indigenes.

This has long been recognised, and has been repeatedly recognised by the Courts of the Territory, and by the High Court of Australia. **These rights are a practical equivalent to our concept of ownership.**

Native customary title to land was preserved. A large proportion of the land of value and use in the Territory to which the Administration and Europeans now have or claim title was originally purchased from indigenes, in Papua by the Administration and in New Guinea in part by the New Guinea Company, an organisation which for a time administered that Territory.

These "purchases" in a number of cases have been held by judicial tribunals to

be invalid. Generally speaking there was no concept in native custom or experience of the permanent alienation of land from the clan group by sale or otherwise. The language difficulties were great. The price was paid in goods such as axes and cloth. The ascertaining of the correct group and correct members of the group having customary rights to the land being purchased was often rough and ready.

Because of legislation it is now in many cases impossible and in the rest most difficult for indigenes to challenge such "purchases" and assert their customary rights before any impartial tribunal. This may be convenient and justified, but it should not be lost sight of in understanding the pressures leading to direct action.

SEPTEMBER NEWS ITEMS

A lad, William Walsh, was convicted of robbery **in the Childrens' Court of Victoria twenty years ago**. Since then, he has worked on the wharves. Recently, he was elected to the State's Upper House, and is **now an MLC**....

His criminal record was brought to light, and the case went to three Supreme Court judges. They found that since he is **a past felon, he was now disqualified from sitting in the Upper Chamber**. Victorian Trade Unions are angry about this, and so too are many public figures....

The question is whether **a person, convicted as a minor, should be barred for life** from a particular office? He would be eligible for a Federal position in the Senate, but not for the Victorian Upper House.

What do you think?

Back to William Walsh above. Attempts to rapidly change the law in his favour failed. But he did **gain a seat in the Lower House,** and held it for 13 years from 1979 to 1992.

Fear in the air. September 8th. Four acts of terror were reported at once today. **Two planes** were hijacked by the Palestinian Liberation Forces, and the combined 320 passengers are being held as captives in Jordan....

A third lies in ruins at Cairo airport, where it was blown up after releasing its 197 passengers. **A fourth** returned to London, where it landed with **one** of two hijackers **dead on board**. The surviving terrorist was a Palestinian girl, **Leila Khalid** who was held in London...

World reaction is said to be "a mixture of revulsion, impotent rage and despair, bordering on panic."

Authorities are amazed **that detection systems** at Amsterdam, Zurich, London and Frankfurt **allowed the guerillas to enter the planes carrying weapons.**

Three days later. Another airliner, with 145 passengers, was hijacked and flown to the pirates' airstrip in Jordan. The "commandos" are demanding the immediate release of Leila Khalid.

Two days later the three planes in Jordan were blown up, and 90 women and children were released. The next day, 230 male passengers were released. 40 were still being held. **They were later released** in exchange for half a dozen guerillas previously captured. **Leila Khalid was part of this swap**.

Comment. This saga kept the world breathless for over a week. Everyone was relieved that so few people were killed. Air traffic took a dent for a while.

PULL YOUR HEAD IN

Letters, E Gibb. May I, through your paper, make an appeal to women to show good manners and courtesy by restraining their hair-styles when attending the theatre. The wearing of exaggerated bouffant styling, sometimes extending four to six inches above, and three inches each side of, the head, makes it impossible for those sitting behind to have a clear view of the stage.

As a small child, my grandmother took me often to matinee at a time when ladies wore very large hats, the theatre managements always added a line in their programs which read, "The Management respectfully requests ladies to remove their hats." Unfortunately, you cannot remove a woman's hair, although when one has paid $12.40 to see a famous ballet company, only to sit behind an outsize, vulgar hairdo, one is very tempted to use a sharp pair of scissors!

SOME THINGS NEVER CHANGE

Comment. People around me often complain that the pace of life is too fast, and things keep changing all the time. When I hear this, **I am tempted to point to my book on 1945** when the entire world was persistently rocked with really major events.

But I bite my tongue and say nothing.

On the other hand, there are a multitude of matters that **never** change. Below is one of them.

Letters, Pat Hailstone. I am complaining about the car-parking charges at the air terminal at Mascot. I consider these fees exorbitant and think the public should be made aware that it is being exploited in this regard.

I drove out there to farewell a relative and was forced to pass through a barrier into the compulsory car park as there was nowhere else to go. Three hours later exactly I returned to my car and had to spend about five minutes in a queue with the motor running in order to check out. I was charged a total of 80c, i.e. at the rate of 20c per hour. When I queried this fantastic sum I was told I was five minutes over the hour, and that would cost me another 20c - an expensive five minutes!

I contend that it is wrong to compare parking fees at the new airport with city parking, for the following reasons:

There is no alternative but to use the compulsory car park and no choice but to pay whatever is asked at the gate.

People do not visit an airport for fun or a shopping spree but mainly in the line of duty to farewell or welcome a relative or friend, staying no longer than is necessary.

Visitors to an airport often have to spend a lengthy time waiting around due to factors entirely beyond their control.

THE SILENT MAJORITY

Here is a little contribution that is curious.

> **Letters, D McPherson.** The great pseudo-discovery of the twentieth century has been that of the existence of the silent majority - a supposed great reservoir of rectitude and virtue which by its very existence is the bulwark of democracy and the guarantor of human progress.
>
> Historically, of course, the situation is almost exactly the reverse; it has not been this silent majority but the vocal minority to whom we are indebted for such ethical progress as man has achieved.
>
> The silent majority let Socrates drink the hemlock and sat down to watch Christ dying on the Cross. In Roman arenas it turned thumbs down on the martyrs. In tens of thousands, it flocked to the Crusades, thereby guaranteeing the extinction of its own religion in the lands of its origin.

During the Reformation it accepted Martin Luther's dictum that it is no sin to kill the peasants. In the Germany of a mere quarter-century ago Hitler's "final solution" to "the Jewish problem" was made possible by its slavish obedience.

In these latter days, it flocks to the ballot box, smug in the anonymity democracy gives it, to vote for the politician who has promised to put more money back into its pockets. But when the charity collector calls it searches for the smallest coin it can decently give.

It is indifferent to the fate of any who dares maintain that reverence for life and the conscience of the individual should be the pre-eminent personal and political values. To this silent majority, morality equates with complete acquiescence to the will of the political group in power.

God grant that I may never be numbered as one of the silent majority!

Comment. What is there to say? I **could** say "So What?" But no, I will say nothing. Ironic, isn't it! ,

VANDALISING OF WAR MEMORIALS

Letters, (Mrs) N Lees. It grieved me very much to read of the desecration of the war memorial in Wahroonga Park.

The near relatives of the deceased soldiers are the ones hurt by an act such as this. If it had not been for those brave men who gave their all when they gave their lives, we would have been in the hands of a ruthless, satanic Hitler. My brother, a fine Christian young man, volunteered, to help to save us from a foreign power. His grave is in France.

The majority of the youth of today do not realise what they owe to that generation. They talk about the "generation gap": Do they not realise that almost all of those whose names are on the war memorials were also young men?

The most suitable prayer I can offer for those who deface these memorials is: "God forgive them, for they know not what they do."

All who condone such desecration are equally guilty.

Comment. Remember earlier I mentioned that attendance at Anzac marches had dropped, and I saw that as a sign that respect for things of the past was giving way to a hedonistic drive for more immediate pleasure.

Such vandalism as described above was not just an isolated act. There were often reports of similar incidents, and others. For example, packs of young males and females ganging up on street people and tormenting and injuring them. It seemed that reverence for the old and elderly was less than before, and that Australia was moving into one of its more selfish periods.

Yet, I am happy to say, that right now, at about 2020, the respect for Diggers appears to be greater than ever before. Look at the crowds that attend ANZAC marches. Young and old, Asian or white, Aborigine or not, they all turn out at dawn ceremonies here and abroad. Anzac Day, more sober than ever, is seen as a great Oz holiday, but with the fun suppressed early in solemn tributes to the fallen.

POOR TREATMENT OF VETERANS

But back to 1970. I give below another example of the lowered status of deserving people. I refer to ex-Servicemen who are unfortunate to be in so-called Repatriation Hospitals. These veterans have served their nation under arms, returned alive, but often crippled, and have fallen on hard times. They are in special hospitals reserved for them, and are left there, with little attention paid to them, and with no prospects of getting out and enjoying a wider life.

The Letter below makes a plea on their behalf, and draws attention to the treatment gulf compared to **civilian** mental patients.

Letters, (Rev) R Meyer, Church of England Chaplain, Callan Park Hospital. What I evidently failed to get across was that the 400 men in the Repatriation sections of Callan Park Hospital, the only one I know from long experience, are actually deprived of treatment to an extent that would not be tolerated in a State psychiatric hospital in Sydney.

Allow me to illustrate this. Modern psychiatric treatment calls for a multi-discipline approach. Accordingly, the Health Department provides some 40 doctors and psychiatrists, about 12 social workers, about 12 occupational therapists (numbers change quickly), about six clinical psychologists and four chaplains, all of whom are full-time. This fine team of trained people, together with far greater numbers of dedicated nurses, are provided to treat say 1,100 patients on the civilian side of Callan Park.

The Repatriation Department provides the services of one psychiatrist who also is a Deputy Medical Superintendent of the whole hospital, one medical officer when one can be persuaded into working in an area where treatment is frowned upon, one part-time social worker, a depleted nursing team and nobody else. They are advertising for a clinical psychologist, if one can be persuaded join such a dead-end service.

Yet the Repatriation Department lavishes large sums on constant alterations to its eight-ward buildings and facilities.

One example of enlightened treatment of the Repatriation variety should suffice. There is a notice on the patients' notice board in one alcoholics' ward (it will be removed if this letter is printed) which actually tells these alcoholic Diggers who deserve better treatment, the hours that they are permitted to go to the local hotels for drinking purposes. Nurses will tell you about the scenes of violence that occur most nights when the patients under this treatment get home after 10pm fighting drunk.

Comment. You can see what I mean. These are men who are battlers. They have fallen by the wayside, but their gallantry served this nation well in times of crisis. **They deserve better.** But clearly, they have no political clout, and the nation is happy to turn a blind eye.

THREE LETTERS ON FAMILIAR PROBLEMS

All three of these Letter appeared on the one day, in the *SMH*. This was no special day, just a typical day, and I could go to the same page tomorrow and find another three. They remind us that **the irritations of every-day life were as common then, as they are 50 years later**.

Letters, M Crawford. Regarding Kingsford Smith international airport: It must be distressing for any family arriving at this beautiful facility to have to undergo the trials of handling their own baggage from the distributing turntable through Customs, then to arrive outside and face the prospect of trying to get a taxi.

Conditions are chaotic, to say the least. I would suggest that the minister arrange for one of his assistants to accompany through Customs a female assistant with babe in arm and several youngsters plus usual baggage, and see just what conditions are like.

Customs officers are courteous, but the taxi problem is appalling; there does not appear to be any system. My wife and I waited for over half-an-hour while people with little baggage simply rushed in ahead.

Letters, (Mrs) M Edwards. I disagree with A Vincent about the Maritime Services Board's restrictions regarding people living on boats moored at marinas. He says that the Board's action of limiting living on boats at marinas to three days discriminates against the few.

In the Northbridge area, people living on waterfrontages near the baths are not permitted to have septic tanks at their boatsheds (no sewerage is available). Yet people are living on boats and discharging untreated sewerage into the water. Our family has had more than one proof of this in the baths themselves.

Letters, A Fergusson. Do city dwellers realise just how frustrating living in the country can be when we have to rely on writing to Sydney for information on various matters? Since last October, I have written four letters to one department in Sydney and have so far received no reply. A friend of mine has just told me of a similar experience. In her case it could involve the loss of $70 or more if she does not hear soon.

It is not always economically possible to travel to Sydney and deal with the matter personally although this is the only way we have found of getting results in some cases.

What we need is some contact - some reliable country-service office which will make the inquiries for us at a nominal cost. Do any readers know of such an office?

Comment. The last Letter helps make the point that country living, despite the idyllic picture often painted, also has its complaints.

HOW NAIVE CAN YOU GET?

The following discussion on drugs shows how far the drug scene has moved in fifty years.

Letters, A Gordon, Executive Director, Drug Referral Centre. Figures at our centre show that for every person who started on marihuana, two started on stimulants. In the immature, either may progress under the pressure of pedlars, friends or normal maturation problems, to other drugs.

May I suggest a scale of more common drugs in the order of their psychological producing properties:-

(1) Alcohol, (2) narcotics (including the synthetics), (3) barbiturates and other sedatives, (4) stimulants, (5) analgesics and finally (6) cigarettes, (7) marihuana and (8) tea or coffee.

When taken to excess each of the above has proven physical ill-effects in man, mouse and monkey.

Now, as physical addiction to narcotics is treated medically with another drug with high dependent properties to ease the physical symptoms of withdrawal, it seems to me that under controlled conditions "pot" could be used to reduce psychological dependence.

Such a research program would complement the recently announced project of the Drug Addiction Foundation of Ontario, Canada, whose research aim is into the long and short-term effects of marihuana smoking.

Finally if MB, BS, is speaking as a medical man, he must know that moodiness ("depression") is, per se, a normal reaction to the stresses of growing-up, the onset of a cold or the after-effects of a late night. Equally, elation can follow a social success or the anticipation of a good time to come. The last thing parents should be invited to do is spy on their children.

Parents should realise that their children are young adults and are encouraged to have opinions of their own. The best families are those that trust each other and, even more important, are able to discuss freely and openly with each other such subjects as politics, religion, sex or drugs.

Comment. The hard synthetic drugs, that have developed since, dwarf the worst drugs at the time. And the number of people affected has increased many-fold.

The little homily at the end of the above Letter also shows how very simplistic the world of the writer was. In fact, Mr Gordon was the Executive Director of a big Drug Referral Centre in Sydney, and I was surprised at how little appreciation he showed for the future developments in drugs.

In any case, we all realise that the problem we had, then seemingly large, was kids' stuff compared to what it is now.

ABORIGINAL LAND CLAIMS

Letters, E Heine. It was with utter disgust and dismay that I watched on television the arrest of our Aborigines and others as they demonstrated for justice and land rights for the Gurindjis in the Northern Territory.

If it is right to take this land we call our own without compensation to the Aboriginal, then it would be right for some other nation to take over now.

The United States has at last compensated the natives of Alaska to the extent of millions of dollars and huge tracts of land, and in the name of justice we should do exactly that - our shame has been with us long enough.

Australian society throughout the 1960's had progressively become more sympathetic to the depressed plight of Aborigines. The Aborigines had at the same time become aware of the rights denied them, and were starting to ask for changes. One such change was to claim that vast tracts of land should revert from the white man back to the black.

This might mean that a tract would be controlled by the blacks and developed with white man's capital in conjunction with the whites. Or it might mean that full ownership of the land would pass to blacks, to do whatever they pleased. The claims were at the embryonic stage and were often still just "bright ideas".

But they were there and growing. The Gorton Government would scarcely consider them, But in just two years, Labor's Gough Whitlam would burst on to the scene, and his policy speech announced a determination that land grants should be given. Then, after his election, both the Governments and the Courts saw to it that Aborigines did in fact get a growing series of determinations in their favour. These determinations are still being made to this very day.

FIJI GETS INDEPENDENCE

Fiji is about to gain **its independence from Britain**. It will be self-governing, and no longer a British colony. It will stay in the British Commonwealth of Nations. **Prince Charles** was on hand in Fiji to celebrate with natives. At an out-door ceremony, **they cheered as he sank a long draught of kava.**

OCTOBER NEWS ITEMS

After deliberations, **Cabinet has decided to prosecute** 50 young men who **refused to register for National Service....**

Prosecutions **had** been suspended while an attempt was made to find suitable civilian alternatives. This **attempt has been abandoned** as being impractical....

It is reported that this sample of 50 is just **the tip of the iceberg**.

For the last 20 years there had been some success in **reducing the open enmity between the Catholic and other Christian Churches world-wide.** The attitude of the reformers was that while they we have differences, they both shared the same Christian God, and the **focus should be on what they had in common**, rather than on their differences....

So **it came as a shock** to many when the **Anglican Archbishop of Sydney**, Reverend Sloane, said that **he would not join the Pope in a common service** in Sydney later this year. The cause of ecumenism, actively seeking peace between Christian Churches, **suffered a setback that upset many Christians**.

The very first jumbo jet put down in Sydney on October 4th. It was a Boeing 747, carrying 312 passengers. Despite being 10 hours behind schedule, **it was greeted by crowds "of thousands".**

Canberra is often described as a dead city where **nothing happens**. But it joined the real world today. The National Bank was **robbed in the Capital's first hold-up.**

The Pope's impending visit has a lot of Protestant clergy very worked up. For example, one prominent minister has requested that Reverend **Ian Paisley** of Ireland visit here at the same time. Paisley is a Protestant leader and **rabble-rouser in his home nation**, and riots often follow his public meetings...

Prime Minister Gorton has decided that Paisley **will not be granted a visa to enter Australia during the Pope's visit**. He explains that this is **to preserve law and order**, on the evidence that Paisley so often promotes violence in religion-torn Ireland.

The Westgate Bridge over the Yarra collapsed into the River this morning. 34 people are known to have died, although only 18 have as yet been identified among the rubble. Eighteen others were injured and four workmen were missing....

A 2,000-ton span, 384 yard long, fell 150 feet into the river. Two riggers fell with the span and were pulled unconscious from the water. Others were not so lucky and were crushed to death under the mountain of steel and concrete debris.

YOUR CLEAN BOOK WILL NOT SELL

The Letter below comes from Judy Keneally, the wife of renowned Australian author Thomas. It follows the raving success of a book called *Portnoy's Complaint* that had just been banned by various State and Commonwealth censors.

Penguin Books defied the ban in an undercover way, and three States decided that it should be released. So after a year, it was generally available in bookstores, provided it was not displayed, and provided that customers asked specifically for the book.

But back to Judy Keneally. Her husband had not yet reached the fame that was later his. Her plaintive Letter struck a chord with anyone who has ever tried to sell books.

> **Letters, J Keneally.** It was my husband's bad or good fortune to have had a novel of his issued by Penguin books the day after the issue of "Portnoy's Complaint."
>
> As far as I know, my husband's novel did not sell 75,000 copies on its first day of issue, this failure being partially due, I feel, to the indifference of the Chief Secretary and the police to local writers. Though my husband is not a pornographer of any standing and has failed to be banned even in Ireland, he did manage to use a four-

letter word participially in his last novel, and should surely be given credit as a trier.

I suggest, therefore, a pornography tariff for the native-born Australian writer, by which, for example, one four-letter word written by an Australian is worth at least four imported four-letter words. Only by some such means can the local writer become subject to that brand of official attention which will guarantee him a large scale.

TO BE OR NOT TO BE

Abortion continued to be a topic for dispute. The arguments that support it or oppose it were pretty much the same, and in the long run, come down to when does a foetus become a human being. If you decide that a foetus at such and such a time becomes a human, then if you then remove it after that, you are committing murder. **There are all sorts of equivocations and twists and turns to this statement**, but that was the essence of the debates that continued to rack society.

I give you three typical Letters expressing the current gyrations in opinions. Notice that they all express **strong opinions, but do not get even close to a persuasive argument.**

Letters, J Freebury, President, Abortion Law Reform Association (NSW). Speaking in the General Assembly of the Presbyterian Church, Dr McPheat said: "A woman desiring an abortion was suffering from fatigue and shock and was not in a position to make a decision."

Absolute rot! How would he know how the majority of women feel - why aren't women who know ever asked their opinion?

I have been told this story before by a clergyman... the women who approached him (four to be exact in 30 odd years) felt some emotional trouble. One must not forget the fact that these particular women were probably suffering from psychiatric disturbances in the first instance, or perhaps, just felt the need to talk the matter over with somebody of the church.

Dr P Tarnesby said in his book "Abortion" (written after the first year of the UK Act), "It is not our experience to find serious psychiatric disturbances after abortion more commonly than one might expect in the population generally."

Letters, W McPheat, St Andrew's Presbyterian Church, Brisbane. Julia Freebury dismisses a statement on abortion attributed to me during the general assembly of the Presbyterian Church as "absolute rot."

The statement as reported was: "A woman desiring an abortion was suffering from fatigue and shock and was not in a position to make a decision."

Two comments:

(i) What I said was that many women at the time when they make a decision on a possible abortion (usually between the 6th and 8th weeks of pregnancy, or a little later) were in a state of fatigue, nausea and possibly depression. Frequently, if helped by advice and medication at this stage and persuaded to carry on for a month or two, they experienced a quite remarkable change of heart. From being unplanned and unwanted, the baby became unplanned but very much wanted.

(ii) My authority for making this observation was not simply my personal experience, but the judgment of many physicians of eminent standing. In Brisbane recently Lady Cilento, calling on over 50 years of general medical practice, presented convincing evidence that this factor should not be overlooked.

Abortion raises complex moral and practical issues. It is to be hoped Julia Freebury and her association do not emotively dismiss all evidence not in accord with their views.

Letters, A Macken. Mrs Julia Freebury again advances her claims for legalised abortion.

Human life must be protected by the fullest possible enforcement of the law - especially when it is most helpless and dependent.

At no stage of a child's existence should parents have absolute rights over it. The law relating to abortion, unlike that dealing with prostitution or homosexuality, is not merely a law of moral prohibition.

This is a law to protect the most basic human right, to life itself - guardianship of which is the very touchstone of law.

This new life a woman shelters is not hers or part of her own body. From its beginning, the foetus is its own person. Its existence may pose problems for the mother and for society, but smashing this new person solves nothing in the long run.

Our society needs to improve the quality of life, but not by destroying life itself. Surely we have advanced beyond this?

DOORKNOCK APPEALS

Here are two different approaches to door-knock appeals for funds.

Letter, (Rev) J Helm. Last Sunday I spent the afternoon with a number of people knocking on doors for the Freedom from Hunger Campaign. I am moved to comment on a fact which has become apparent in doorknocks over the years - the bigger the house, the smaller the donation.

This, of course, is a simplification of the situation, but a reasonable summary. We covered a segment of Mosman which has several blocks of luxury home units and many of the stately homes of the district. Almost without exception the paper donations came from those in modest circumstances, while the single coin or the outright refusal often came from those who have so much.

What a pity it is that affluence so often seems to make a person less sensitive to the needs of others. May I use your column to remind our nation that wealth carries with it great responsibilities, and that the way we respond to an appeal such as the Freedom from Hunger Campaign reveals our attitude to all of life?

Letter, Tony Alfreds. There is no authority that controls door-knock appeals. There are laws that prevent beggars in the streets, and in some States, there are laws that protect for soliciting by vagrants.

But, nothing that saves the householder from being plagued by collectors from charities who feel they can righteously invade a house and put the occupant on the spot for a donation.

Since about 1960, the number of Appeals that come to my door has grown and grown. Some of them are fair dinkum, and some of them are just fakes organised by criminals. All they need is nice clothing, a card that looks nice, a fancy name for a mythical charity, a log-book to record donations. It helps if they have a pretty face, and are female as well.

They have got to plague proportions. No wonder donations in the richer areas have dropped. Over the years, our houses have been targeted, and have been visited time and again by bogus collectors. I am sick of it. If I had my way, I would train all dogs to bite on sight of anyone with an identification badge or card.

Comment. Somewhere along the line, authorities in various States have ruled that charities **must be licensed** to approach homes, and that the number of such charities is limited.

The Letter from Mr Alfreds convince me that this is a good thing.

PIE-EATERS

Letters, S Last. It seems as though pie orders for Vietnam go astray. My lad, 2792647 Pte Ken Last of 8 RAR, was commissioned to take back four dozen pies when returning from R and R last month. I ordered them for him - somehow they went astray.

In order not to disappoint the members of 4th Platoon, "B" Coy, the managing director of Gartrell White had the pies consigned to my lad free of charge. They arrived in good condition. However, they were covered in ants before being eaten. The comment by the lads was: "We've eaten worse than this out on patrol, and if an ant gets in the way that's its bad luck."

Comment. This is a reminder that we were then, at least, **a nation of pie-eaters**. It leads me to ask what Mum would send to a soldier fighting in Vietnam today. A chicken kebab? A green salad with plenty of lettuce?

MORE THEATRE ANTICS TO BEWARE

A few pages back, I published a Letter that talked about the perils of sitting behind women with large hair-dos in the theatre.

Another reader, inspired by the above, added to the list of irritants.

> **Letters, (Miss) E Pender.** Now that the Barenboim feast is over for Sydney, I should like to record a word of praise for the audiences, which on the whole responded superbly to his artistry and paid him the compliment of complete silence during the performances.
>
> Generally, the people who sit near me at concerts (or do they sit near everyone?) turn my mild nature into one of murderous ferocity. They beat time with fingers or feet, snatch up programs and turn pages (what do they hope to find?), wear suede coats (they squeak), hold plastic or patent leather handbags (they pop), scratch, with rasping sound, their stockings (women) or chins (men).
>
> The list is endless, and when the Opera House is finished, with its more sophisticated acoustics, every ticking watch will be a hazard! As with guns in the Wild West, the management might arrange to have them left at the door.

RELIGIOUS WARS

Reverend Sloane's refusal to join with the Pope stirred up old hatreds, and re-ignited the thirst for blood in the ranks of clergy. Before looking at some opinions, let me preface by saying that almost all letters started by saying that it was a matter of personal opinion as to whether Sloane attended, and that they respected his right, or anyone else's, to do as he chose. Only after did they go for the jugular.

Letters, (Miss) W Amies, P Wotton (St James); R Hoddinott (St Alban's); D Davies (St Peter's); S Churches (St Paul's College); M Perrott (Christ Church St Laurence); F Collis (St Anne's). We, the undersigned, deplore the attitude of the Anglican Archbishop of Sydney towards the coming visit of His Holiness Pope Paul.

As Anglicans, we can only say to our Roman Catholic brethren that this decision is far from representative of the views of the great majority of the Anglican Communion. The Diocese of Sydney is unique throughout the world for its brand of Anglicanism and seeming intolerance towards the Roman Catholic Church, with whom the Anglican Church has so many common bonds.

Letters, G Evans and Eight Others. We endorse the stand that the Archbishop of Sydney has taken on the Pope's visit.

It must be realised that the Archbishop has taken his stand on Biblical and doctrinal truth and that while the doctrines which divide the Anglican Church from the Roman Catholic Church exist, there will continue to be this division. We must not risk compromising what we believe to be the truth for the sake of ecumenism.

We believe there can be no compromise as far as the Scriptural truth on which our Church is founded is concerned.

News Item. The executive of the Baptist's Union of NSW said that the 200 Baptist clergy of NSW should not take part in the ecumenical service .The spokesman said that it was not a matter of bigotry, intolerance,and bitterness, but rather a deep difference in the ways that the two religions saw fit to serve their God.

Letters, Fay Coutts. I have no interest at all in who goes where with the Pope, but I noticed a Letter that was full of bigotry, intolerance and bitterness, and I hope that the person who wrote it is never in a position to influence the minds of others.

News item. A prominent Methodist, Dr Udi, stated that Sloane was "ecumenically myopic" and this sent several ministers spinning trying to recant that statement.

Comments. The Letters went on and on. Pages of them, all very long, very often quoting some sections of the Bible, always picking quotations that clashed with each other, and full of a vicious sanctity that only Australian clergy can muster.

Comment. As I re-read the above, I realise I have been hard on the clergy. They are better-intentioned than my words suggest, and are truly dedicated and Christian in almost all things.

But over the twenty years of writing these Books, I have seen that every time a religious issue surfaces, they come out in an absolutely partisan way and advocate the party line as if there is not one of them who can think outside the indoctrination handed down to them.

Second Comment. Will I erase the above comments, as being unnecessarily argumentative? Probably not. I think you can handle this. But if they are not there when you come to read this book, I suggest you ignore them.

NOVEMBER NEWS ITEMS

42 persons in Paris were burned to death when a dance hall caught fire and burned to the ground.

A labourer, working at the silos in Newcastle's Carrington, was loading bags of wheat dust onto a truck. He felt good, and **was loading two bags at a time....**

Another worker objected to this on the basis that he **was working too hard, and reducing the number of jobs available to others**. They came to blows, and the **labourer was knocked unconscious.** The other worker was admonished and fined by the Court.

A **Western Australian horse** *Clear Prince* is firming as favourite for the **Melbourne Cup**. I will bring you the result if space allows.

The newish Leader of the Labor Party, **Gough Whitlam**, is gradually making a name for himself. Right now he **is advocating strongly for the immediate removal of all troops from Vietnam**....

This is equally **strongly opposed** by Gorton. And by a Liberal up-and-comer called **Malcolm Fraser**....

I have **a feeling** that Whitlam and Fraser will clash over other issues in future. **But, no. That is just silly talk. Take no notice of it.**

Two experimental radar road traps will start up today in NSW. **Their use will be extended to other regions if they are found to reduce road deaths....**

They were tried across Australia from 1959, but were discarded because it was found that reflections made them **unreliable**. Since then, improvements have been made.....

South Australia had used them generally for a decade. **Queensland** uses them on roads that are posted so that motorists will be aware of their presence.

The horse of a grazier, from Finley, near Melbourne, fell and was crippled. The rider broke his pelvis and leg, and could not get his foot from the stirrup for 20 minutes. He found he could not walk. **He had to crawl a mile back to his home.....**

The grass was very long and he could not see where he was headed. He crawled past his house a long way, and he had to double back. **So he took three days** to make the journey....

On the extremely painful crawl, he was dying from thirst. His dog went for a swim in an irrigation channel, and when he returned, **the grazier licked his fur to get enough water for him to survive**. He is recovering in Mooroopna Hospital.

THE TAMBORINE BRIGADE

The Hare Krishna movement was a form of Hinduism that showed up in society here about 1970. My general impression of followers in our capital cities were that they were non-violent, they did not eat meat, and they wore long flowing garbs and the men had long unkempt hair. And the women were pushy and loud-mouthed.

They had a bad reputation for ganging together in the streets, and pushing themselves on people passing by, and aggressively pestering them for money. Put this together, and you get the impression that they were a pretty nasty lot.

But, I suspect that this view was not correct. Certainly, the view expressed below speaks differently of them.

Letters, W Gunderson, Hare Krishna Movement. A short mention of our religious organisation was printed in your Column Eight, or at least the vague description of the same. We are offended to have read the description of us as a "quasi-religious sect dunning strollers to buy their tracts - at 50c each."

Ours is not a make-show or pretentious organisation. We have centres in every major city of the world and our lineage of Spiritual Perceptors is the oldest and most revered throughout India, called by the name Madhya Goudyia (Brahma) Sampradaya. We are practising Vaishnavas or Devotees of the Lord God (God is One for the Christians, Jews, Moslems and Hindus etc). Our life is regulated to strict principles and our aim is to purify the ever-increasing Godless atmosphere by simple singing of God's Holy Name in the public areas.

We distribute our sound magazine for any donation no matter how small, and if there is a sincere soul who desires it but cannot afford to give a donation then the magazine is freely given to that person. We are always congenial and ready to answer any questions of any passerby.

My purpose in writing you is to let you know exactly what we are doing, and why, and who we are. As I mentioned above we live by strict principles. The gist of which are:

(1) We take no intoxicants (including coffee, tea or cigarettes).

(2) We live a life of self-restraint and celibacy unless bound by legal and spiritual marriage for purpose of raising god-conscious children.

(3) We don't gamble.

Our schedule is to rise between 3.30am and 4am, to maintain hygiene and practise devotions (this includes public glorification of God) eating only one main meal in a day. We have many duties and we take our rest at 10pm. We are basically good, sincere people as anyone who makes an effort to find out will see.

My humble request is to have you print this letter in the next issue of your fine newspaper. This will let people know a little about this unusual "chanting sect" that has come to Sydney to distribute freely what most of have forgotten: pure Love of God!

Comment. I **accept** that the movement was better than the brief summary I gave above, I **accept** that its worldwide popularity at the time shows a love of their God which led them to strive for better lives and goals. My own impression of them was gained from thrice having to push through a small group of them to get to my Sydney office. And that left a bias against them.

In any case, they were active in our capital cities for a decade and, for most people, they never gained the acceptance or popularity that they hoped for. But the final straw for them came in 1978.

The Hilton Hotel in Sydney was the venue for a big international gathering of politicians from round the British Commonwealth world. It was a so-called CHOGM meeting. The security was tight. Still, in a garbage bin outside the Hilton, a bomb exploded and killed three people and badly injured eight others.

One of the major suspects was the Ananda Marga movement, though there was never any real evidence of that. But this movement was similar in appearance and behaviour to the Hare Krishna cult. Both of them were tarred with the same brush, and both of them were in future seen on fewer days about the cities.

MORE PRESSURES ON MOTORISTS

The Roads authorities were trying hard to reduce the road toll. The latest suggestion for trialling was that **seat belts should be made compulsory**. At the moment, some drivers choose to wear them, but it seems likely they would be **made** to wear them all the time in the very near future.

Letters, (Mrs) M Edwards. If the wearing of seat belts in cars is going to become compulsory, could something be done to improve their design?

My car has bucket-type front seats, with hand-brake and gear-shift between them. Every time I want to put my seat belt on I have to dig around on the floor in the back of the car, untangle the thing from around the hand-brake - nine times out of ten it's caught under the seat.

If my husband has been driving the car and has adjusted the belt for his driving position,

I have to alter the setting on the whole contraption, unless I want it across my throat.

Comment. Every time the road rules were made tougher, vocal parts of the population could find lots of arguments against the changes. Yet, after a while, the level of animosity dropped, and sensible people got used to the new regime. And later, when the statistics caught up, it was found that the new rules had been worthwhile after all.

Of course, there are limits to that. If, for example, the authorities decided that alcohol was the cause of road deaths, they might set limits on how much alcohol a driver could have. I have no idea how they would measure that, but suppose they could. Do you think that the population here would stand for that? **Surely it is a god-given right to drink as much as you can, and then drive your own car to where ever you like.**

No, I do not see that happening. Our beer-swilling men and women would **never** allow this to happen. Some things **must** never change.

FLY IN, FLY OUT

One of the consequences of so many people moving to the cities is that the bird-life that once lived in the outer suburbs has now moved further into the bush, and the calls of singing birds are no longer heard.

Correspondence confirming this has been brisk. Most people rue what is happening, though a minority claim that they are better off now without the nuisance of bird droppings.

The currawong has been at the forefront of writers. Three Letters below are typical of the ongoing debate.

Letters, R Strahan, Director, Taronga Zoo. In reference to the killing of currawongs: The currawong is an impressive bird with a delightful call and, like the kookaburra and magpie, it is carnivorous. The flocks which aggregate around Sydney in the winter certainly kill some nestling birds and lizards, but they also account for a number of insects. I am not convinced that they are removing or displacing any birds native to Sydney, and the accusation that they are detrimental to fairy wrens and other small species may be based on a misreading of the evidence.

One often hears it said, particularly by people moving into newer suburbs, that wrens and wagtails were common until the currawongs came. What is overlooked is that the original native scrub and leaf litter provided food and shelter for the small birds and that when this was replaced by lawn and ordered gardens, their life-support system failed. Larger, more wide-ranging and adaptable birds such as currawongs, kookaburras, and magpies remained in the trees.

Letters, D Hudson. I am quite surprised that the Director of Taronga Zoo has such a misty knowledge of the habits of the currawong. I have observed them here for 26 years. Far from there being a "misreading of the evidence," the reports of the currawong are grimly factual.

I have seen the currawong drive away the wren, the honey-eater and even that great Australian, the kookaburra. Ten years ago my area, one of the best in Sydney for birdlife, carried a profusion of all types of birds. Currawongs then decided to nest in the spring in a large Port Jackson eucalyptus. They have returned each year and those of the birds which they have not eaten they have driven out.

In addition to denuding the area of birdlife, they have destroyed my bantam chickens and fouled all my garden furniture, footpaths, etc.

My area has remained unchanged for 26 years and I am particularly annoyed at the eviction of the kookaburras which lived as a colony in the gum trees. We used to feed them personally, by hand.

The currawong is a vicious, aggressive scavenger and is deeply entrenched in the wild country north and west of Sydney. It has no place in Sydney suburbs and to refer to its annoying, monotonous "ka-wok ka-wok" as a "delightful call" is to make a most extraordinary statement, to say the least.

Mr Strahan believes that currawongs congregate around Sydney in flocks in the winter. I invite him to visit my suburb any time in the 365 days of the year, and I will show him this vicious destroyer of the ways and habits of the small and large birdlife of Australia.

But there is another side to this story.

Letters, Norton Small. My heart goes out to the city dwellers because they are driving out birds from their minute back-yards. There is one solution if they really want to have birds live around them. Move to the country.

That is too sensible for city folks. But they can console themselves with the thought that when birds are driven out of the city, they go and live in the country.

So, the country benefits by pikers going to the city. On balance, then, we in the country have the choice of keeping our city-bound pikers, or getting more birds.

This is not an even choice. I'll take the birds anytime.

RAW POLITICS

Towards the end of November, an election will be held for the Senate. That means that half the existing Senate will retire, and another group will replace it. It does not have the immediate impact of a House of Representatives election, but it gives a good indication of how the Parties are going.

The Labor Party seems to be in a better position than it has been for years. Of course, it still has its wrangles, and sackings, and factions, and it has the Trade Unions interfering and trying to run the whole joint. But it always has these things.

What is different is that many of the old hands, who have been leading the Party for 30 years, have now gone. In their place, the new leader, Gough Whitlam, has done a good job in setting strong policies, and bullying his executives in the many State Branches to follow him. He is a force to be reckoned with.

The Liberals, on the other hand, appear to be wandering. Their policies seem to be to maintain the status quo in most areas. Since John Gorton took over as Prime Minister, there have been no popular policy moves, just a um-drum policy of keeping going on the same path.

So, I predict that Labor will come out of the election with an increased vote. Not necessarily with more Senate **seats**. But, yes, more **votes** than before.

THE ELECTION RESULT

Both Parties lost votes, but Labor lost more than the Liberals. The DLP (Catholic backed) picked up the votes that the Major Parties lost. Liberals lost one seat. **While Labor picked up two.** The Liberals no longer have a majority in the Senate.

ALL FIRED UP

The **eight volunteer firemen** at Injune, 200 miles west of Brisbane, **resigned last night** after their dilapidated equipment failed and **their superintendent's cafe burned down.**

DECEMBER NEWS ITEMS

The Pope is in Australia. On his way here, **in Manila**, a would-be **assassin**, dressed as a priest, waited at the foot steps of the plane, and then **lunged at the Pope** with a 12-inch knife. His hand hit the Pope's chest, but **no harm was done to hisHoliness.** Others were cut somewhat. ....

The would-be killer said he wanted to kill to **save the people from hypocrisy and superstition**. He is being held in custody in a secret location **to avoid lynching** from strongly Catholic crowds....

The Pope was greeted in Sydney with all **the near-hysteria** that you would expect. In the evening, he celebrated a "glittering Mass" with 4,000 clergymen. **This was replayed on TV next morning**, along with sporting replays....

The next day, he again said Mass before **a crowd of 250,000 at Randwick racecourse**. Then, next day, the **ecumenical service was held** at the Sydney Town Hall. 2,500 persons of all denominations attended. **Dr Sloane did not attend....**

The Pope flew out after a full three-day visit. At the airport were Cardinal Gilroy, the PM, the GG, the NSW Governor and the Premier.

The **Minister for Customs and Excise** said that parents would be stupid if they thought that the Government or the Drug Squad **could save their children from drugs. "The consumption of drugs has risen 20 times in the last two years"**. He was referring to marihuana and hashish as the drugs under discussion. **He hinted darkly at LSD** and other drugs three times stronger than anything we had ever seen.

A Papuan has been appointed to head the Papua-New Guinea Public Service Board.

A prolonged battle is expect to start over the manning of **one-man double decker buses.** Unions are conscious that **these buses will reduce the need for conductresses,** and management think the same. Both parties are talking about the benefits and risks for passengers and staff. But **that is all smoke screens**, and the issue is over **employment and Union power.**

Extra radar units will be deployed at **random spots on the roads in NSW.** Previously, they were used at marked spots **at permanent sites.** They will also be deployed **outside the metropolitan areas**....

The addition of three new units will bring the **total in NSW to up to five. The two permanent units had shown a very positive effect**....

Police add that, though the number of units is currently small, they expect that soon the State will be **"saturated with them"**.

MERRY CHRISTMAS - IF POSSIBLE

Every year, at about this time, women citizens of this often-sensible nation spend a month running round like hens, clucking and making life merry for others over the so-called Christmas period.

During this period, I normally put a sign up on my lawn that says "Sadly, Deceased." Some years if I am feeling expansive, the sign reads "Sadly, Very Deceased". The obvious aim is to deter visitors and other well-wishers from pushing their "Merry Christmases" on me.

You get the point. I do not like Chrismas and all the drinking and eating and presents and kids screaming "gimme". Over many years, in my books, I have said this in all sorts of ways, so I will not dwell on it again. And, I know that most readers do get a kick out of Christmas. So, now I will behave myself, and drop the Scrooge pose.

I will even go so far as to publish two Christmas Letters. One from a do-gooder and consistent with the Love-thy-neighbour nonsense. (***Stop it. You are knocking Christmas again.*) And the other from a very sensible man who has good values and judgement.**

(*I said, stop it.*)

Letters, P Eerdmans. During the past few weeks I have vainly tried to buy Christmas cards benefiting some worthy cause.

I considered that at obvious places like Martin Plaza, the bigger city banks, Wynyard Station, etc. there would be stalls at this time of the year to sell cards to the many people who would like to see charities benefit in this meaningful way. This is surely the ideal time of the year to assist financially deserving causes, by buying their cards and channeling thousands of dollars to places where this money is badly needed.

I feel certain that many public-spirited citizens would happily volunteer to sell cards for charity, and I am most surprised that this golden once-a-year opportunity is not exploited to the full by the many institutions anxious to raise funds for the causes they serve.

Most of the enormous profits made on the sale of greeting cards should go to the needy elements in our society?

Letters, George Smith. Mr Eerdmanns clearly does not have any experience in Business. If he did he would know that most small businesses in the nation survive only because the owners do not want to do anything else. They run on a budget that covers expenses barely, and just make enough money to live on.

When it comes to Christmas cards, the profit margin is good. But in other parts of the business, the profit margin is not good. Some sales always produce a loss, but the owner carries them to attract more sales of other products.

The profit from Christmas cards is quite important to keep newsagents in the business. Without that profit, they would be marginal, and some of them would go out of business. Then a lot of people would not be so merry at Christmas.

Comment. A woman from the Church Missionary Society added a different plea. She sees church sales of Christmas cards as being necessary to finance the overseas Christian missions. Another writer interjected that the woman might see the missions as a good thing, but that he does not. He sees them as agents for colonialisation, and pushing foreign religions on native populations, most of whom live fuller lives than Christians.

DEATH DUTIES

Many readers will have forgotten that **death duties were still on all statute books in 1970.** They varied form State to State, but about 5 per cent or more of the value of an estate was taken by Governments during the probate process. Many heirs who were assets-rich, but cash-flow poor, were forced to sell assets or the full estate to pay death duties. This was particularly true in rural areas where it forced the selling off of various paddocks to meet the bill.

This voice below is one of the first to oppose the various bits of legislation.

Letters, W Keighley, MLC. Your Column Eight of December 10 seems to evince some surprise at the strength of feeling behind Senator Negus of Western Australia and his **campaign for abolition of death duty**.

There is in the country a belief, to which I subscribe, that death duties are an immoral impost levied in the general belief that they are an easy way of extracting, from relatively few people, a large revenue.

It is my belief that far more people are affected, or feel they are likely to be affected, by death duties than politicians calculate, due (a) to the falling value of money and (b) to the substantial maintenance of duty rates at levels fixed many years ago.

I am of the opinion that were any political party to make an election promise to abolish death duties (succession duties and gift duties with them) it would attract a significant leakage of votes from the other political parties.

Abolition of death duties would bring additional capital inflow, resulting in additional taxable income.

Government expenditure, Federal and State, could be reduced by the use of any reputable industrial consultant, probably with resultant increases in Departmental output.

Other writers raised good issues. Where they asked, is the morality in taking assets away from the beneficiaries of a person who spent their entire life amassing assets only to have them taken away and given to the general population? Can anyone establish that these monies will be spent wisely? Then again, would people keep striving to add to their assets if they can be whisked away from them? Would smarties find legal loopholes to avoid payments? Would everyone, even the poor, be affected? Why would the poor be exempted? After all, they chose to be poor. They already get too may benefits.

In any case, all regimes in the nation have now done away with these taxes. **But, be aware, they can always be brought back.** At some stages, there are groups and factions in political parties that advocate doing just that. If you want to pass on your assets to your own, be vigilant.

WORKING MOTHERS

A debate was building with stay-at-home mothers. The Public Relations Officer of the Nursing Mothers' Association added her bit.

> **Letters, B Sutherland.** We feel that there is a great need for education for parenthood to be included in every school's curriculum so that today's schoolchildren, many of whom will be parents within a few years of leaving school, become aware of the responsibilities associated with bringing children into this world.
>
> Surely it is illogical to lay great stress on the educational qualifications needed for teaching other people's children, for properly trained staff to run nurseries, etc, and then to give young women the idea that looking after their own children is a waste of intellect.
>
> The aims of the Nursing Mothers' Association of Australia are to promote an interest in breast-feeding as a basis for better mothering, and the development of closer and happier family relationships.
>
> Modern social conditions tend to isolate young mothers at the very time when they most need friendly help in raising their families. Economic pressures, problems of combining careers with home duties

are widely experienced. We hold regular discussion groups in members' homes as a means of bringing mothers with similar ideas on child-rearing together in an informal atmosphere.

Thus, we hope to help women work towards that most important cornerstone of our community - the stability of our homes.

The two Letters below do not much address the previous Letter, but show other sides to be considered in the growing controversy. As usual everyone had their own views that were quite valid. As seen from their own viewpoint.

Letters (Mrs) M Diesner. One gets the impression from this article and others like it that housework is such that a woman must resort either to tranquillisers or the burden of two jobs to alleviate its effect.

One reason often given is that housework consists only of a deadly routine. But when one thinks of various highly rated jobs, such as that of a doctor, dentist or airline pilot, one realises that these are also essentially routine. So what's wrong with housework?

The trouble lies in the solitude in which a housewife works. She spends her day in silence, with little chance of making any adult contact. This fact explains to me why married women will travel hours to reach low-paid, boring jobs. Their fares and extra clothes cost as much as the contents of their pay-packet.

One can't do much about the necessity of doing housework alone, but opportunities could be made to give women much-needed human contact across the middle of the day by the widespread provision of part-time employment. If employers only took time to think, they would realise that many full-time jobs in shops, offices, warehouses and laboratories, have only a part-time content.

The employment of housewives - and students - part-time in such positions would lead to greater productivity at work and greater contentment on the home front.

Letters, Mother. Mr Gorton is disturbed that 45,000 working mothers are leaving their children unattended outside school hours.

Having been widowed earlier this year, I certainly wasn't offered a full pension by the Government to enable my 9-year-old daughter to be attended to at all times; and having had a mother to return to from school each afternoon myself, I didn't feel inclined to leave my daughter to fend for herself. So I did the only thing possible: I employed a woman to "mind" my daughter at a cost of 50c an hour.

In a normal school week, this amounts to $8. With school holidays it increases to $11.

Thinking I would be entitled to a tax rebate on child minding, I included the item in my tax return, and in due course was advised that the item was termed private expenditure.

Not being satisfied, I wrote to the Commissioner of Taxation and was advised that the matter had been "noted" and would receive attention as soon as possible.

So I guess that if Mr Gorton was in my position, he would not only be disturbed - he would be very concerned.

SPEECH DAYS

Below is another writer who finds some part of the Christmas ritual a pain the neck. I will show my normal restraint on the Chrismas matter, but I must add that I heartily endorse her view, and find her to be a person of exquisite intelligence.

Letters, SN. I have just returned from our annual ordeal, our daughter's school speech day, and before headmasters and headmistresses begin organising their next year's effort, may I, on behalf of the many thousands of parents frantically endeavouring to cope with the many extra chores expected of them around Christmas, appeal to them to let us off a little lighter next year?

We were obliged to sit through three hours of purgatory. Numerous musical items (admittedly excellent), speeches from a chosen speaker, two local MPs (no less), an over-enthusiastic master of ceremonies, the head of the P and C association, the headmistress's report, the outgoing head-girl and the incoming head-girl - all made speeches. Also, the master of ceremonies had apparently not been told that all he was expected to do was introduce the speakers, for he treated us to an extra speech with each introduction.

One feels that this is all some diabolical plot to make parents pay for their apparent indifference to their children's needs during the year.

Surely it is possible for to have some liaison between the headmistress and the various speakers, so that it was not necessary to endure the continual repetition of what had been done by the various parties concerned in the school welfare, the endless votes of thanks to the same people and the so-often-heard and no-longer-heeded advice to the justifiably wriggling and bored schools.

May I appeal to head teachers to give children and parents a speech day they will look forward to, not dread, at the end of the school year?

SUMMING UP 1970

In writing this book, I did not discuss the economy very much. That is because nothing much happened. It just kept plugging along. There were a few hurdles, like dispute over wool payments, and there were tax increases that were gobbled up by inflation. But nothing to write home to Mum about.

Mind you, in just a couple of years, Britain will join the European Common Market. And we will see that many of our comfortable trade deals with the UK will take a lot of managing. But to some extent we are already moving towards trading with other partners, so the effect of the move will not be too bad.

The Vietnam war was just as bad as last year. But it was clear that the US-led forces, including Australia, had no hope of a military victory. Our allies were scrambling to get out of it, but were trapped by the enthusiasm for war that they had themselves built up when they thought earlier that they could be winners. Now, politically they were caught. Pull out of the war? Admit that it had served no purpose? Not likely. How would they tell **that** to **the families of the dead and maimed**?

Importantly, the nation's safety net was still in place. Pensions, social service payments, public housing, payments to schools and for roads and infrastructure all of these were adequate. No one says they were generous. But adequate, yes.

And what else could you expect? We are a young county, with huge areas. Our infrastructure is vast, our standard of living is high, so that our wages are generous. Everything we do costs a lot. Other, more developed nations simply re-use their old assets. We have to develop them from scratch So benevolence is not yet in our grasp.

But in 1970 we did alright. Our one folly was being in Vietnam where our menfolk were being killed. If we can ignore that, **and we should not**, it has been a pretty good year, and if we can stick it out till the cursed war ends, we can do better next time.

But, for now, **I wish you a Merry Christmas, and all the best for the New Year.**

READERS' COMMENTS

Tom Lynch, Speers Point. Some history writers make the mistake of trying to boost their authority by including graphs and charts all over the place. You on the other hand get a much better effect by saying things like "he made a pile". Or "every one worked hours longer than they should have, and felt like death warmed up at the end of the shift." I have seen other writers waste two pages of statistics painting the same picture as you did in a few words.

Barry Marr, Adelaide. You know that I am being facetious when I say that I wish the war had gone on for years longer so that you would have written more books about it.

Edna College, Auburn. A few times I stopped and sobbed as you brought memories of the postman delivering letters, and the dread that ordinary people felt as he neared. How you captured those feelings yet kept your coverage from becoming maudlin or bogged down is a wonder to me.

Betty Kelly, Wagga Wagga. Every time you seem to be getting serious, you throw in a phrase or memory that lightens up the mood. In particular, in the war when you were describing the terrible carnage of Russian troops, you ended with a ten-line description of how aggrieved you felt and ended it with "apart from that, things are pretty good here". For me, it turned the unbearable into the bearable, and I went from feeling morbid and angry back to a normal human being.

MORE INFORMATION ON THESE BOOKS

Over the past 19 years the author, Ron Williams, has written this series of books that present a social history of Australia in the post-war period. They cover the period for 1939 to 1973, with one book for each year. Thus there are 35 books.

To capture the material for each book, he worked his way through the Sydney Morning Herald and the Age/Argus day-by-day, and picked out the best stories, ideas and trivia. He then wrote them up into about 180 pages of a year-book.

He writes in a simple direct style, he has avoided statistics and charts, and has produced easily-read material that is entertaining, and instructive, and charming.

They are invaluable as gifts for birthdays, Christmas, and anniversaries, and for oldies who are hard to buy for.

These books are available at all major retailers such as Dymocks and Collins. Also at on-line retailers such as Booktopia and Amazon, and your local newsagent.

Over the next few pages, summaries of other books in the Series are presented. A synopsis of all books in the Series is available from www.boombooks.biz

****

THERE ARE 35 TITLES IN THIS SERIES

In 1939. Hitler was the man to watch. He bullied Europe, he took over a few countries, and bamboozled the Brits. By the end of the year, most of Europe ganged up on him, and a phony war had millions of men idling in trenches eating their Christmas turkeys. Back home in Oz, the drunkometer was breathless awaited, pigeon pies were on the nose, our military canteens were sometimes wet and sometimes dry. Nasho for young men was back, Sinatra led his bobby-soxers, while girls of all ages swooned for crooner Bing.

In 1948, there was no shortage of rationing and regulation, as the Labor government tried to convince voters that war-time restrictions should stay. The concept of free medicine was introduced, but doctors (still controlled from Britain) would not co-operate, so that medicines on the cheap were scarcely available to the public. Burials on Saturday were banned. Rowers in Oxford were given whale steak to beat meat rationing.

****

Chrissi and birthday books for Mum and Dad and Aunt and Uncle and cousins and family and friends and work and everyone else.

Don't forget a good read and chuckle for yourself.

In 1957, Britain's Red Dean said Chinese Reds were OK. America avoided balance-of-payments problems by sending entertainers here. Sydney's Opera House will use lotteries to raise funds. The Russians launched Sputnik and a dog got a free ride. A bodkin crisis shook the nation. After the Suez crisis last year, many nations were acting tough. In particular, the Arabs and the Jews were sitting on a tinder box, and the Middle East was on the point of eruption..

In 1958, the Christian brothers bought a pub and raffled it; some clergy thought that Christ would not be pleased. Circuses were losing animals at a great rate. Officials were in hot water because the Queen Mother wasn't given a sun shade; it didn't worry the lined-up school children, they just fainted as normal. School milk was hot news, bread home deliveries were under fire. The RSPCA was killing dogs in a gas chamber. A tribe pointed the bone at Albert Namatjira; he died soon after.

****

*Soft covers f*or each of the years from 1939 to 1973

In 1967, postcodes were introduced, and you could pay your debts with a new five-dollar note. You could talk-back on radio, about a brand new ABS show called "This Day Tonight." Getting a job was easy with unemployment at 1.8 % – better that the 5% 50 years later. Arthur Calwell left at last. Whitlam took his place. Harold Holt drowned, and Menzies wrote his first book in retirement.

In 1969. Hollywood produced a fake movie that appeared to show a few Americans walking on the moon. The last stream train was pensioned off as the Indian Pacific crossed the nation. There are now no Labor governments in office in all Australia, but Laborites should not worry because Paul Keating just got a seat in Canberra. Thousands of people walked the streets in demos against the Vietnam War, and HMAS Melbourne cut a US Destroyer in two. The Poseidon nickel boom made the fortunes of many, and the 12-sided cupro-nickel 50cent coin fled the pockets of our new but ubiquitous jeans.

****

www.ingramcontent.com/pod-product-compliance
Lightning Source LLC
Chambersburg PA
CBHW070729020526
44107CB00077B/2191